AF380465

This book is dedicated
to my mother,
whose character traits
of curiosity and enthusiasm
I fortunately inherited.
For that I am grateful.

Thank you Mom!

Michael Wolf

Small God, Big City

Earth God Shrines in Urban Hong Kong

繁華都市小小神

香港市區中的土地神位

Michael Wolf

Hong Kong University Press

Peperoni Books

Small God, Big City
Earth God Shrines in Urban Hong Kong

Lee Ho Yin and Lynne D. DiStefano
Research by
Katie Cummer, Lynne D. DiStefano and Lee Ho Yin

Introduction

What happens when a small god of rural descent is moved to a big city? This, we thought, could be the idea behind Michael Wolf's photographs of Hong Kong's urban Earth God shrines. But as Wolf clarified, "It's not about the Earth God; it's about the context, about what is happening around the shrines and the ingenuity by which the shrines fit into their surroundings!" The purpose of this essay is therefore not to recount the folklore of the Earth God, or to argue about his place within formal religion. Instead, the focus is on the Earth God's relevance to the modern urban world of Hong Kong. The answer the authors seek in this essay is not who the Earth God is in factual and mythical terms, but *what* the Earth God is to the urban context of Hong Kong.

Identity

Like many Chinese gods, the Earth God goes by a number of names and titles, which makes it all the more confusing for English readers. The most common Romanised name is the Pinyin-based "Tudi," which aptly means "earth and land." If you browse through the endlessly retold stories of the Earth God, you learn that the Earth God is a folk belief that grew out of animism and the traditional practice of beatification of fallen heroes and virtuous people. The most typical representation of the Earth God in urban Hong Kong is in the form of a simple tablet carrying the god's name in six Chinese characters that read in Cantonese as "*mun hau to tei choi shen*,"[1] and translate as "by the doorway is the god who begets wealth from the earth and land." This is often a cause for confusion between Tudi, the Earth God, and Choi Shen, the God of Wealth, who are two different entities playing different roles for believers.

The association of the Earth God with wealth is the legacy of an agrarian past, when the economic well-being of households came directly from farming the land. However, the land-connotes-wealth idea embodied in the Earth God is not common knowledge, and it often leads to the mistaken notion that the Earth God is a bearer of wealth (that is the role of Choi Shen, the God of Wealth). The Earth God is in fact a *guardian* of wealth. To explain it more fully, the Earth God does not bring the fortune for creating wealth as Choi Shen does, he simply guards the accumulated wealth and protects it from loss through misfortune. This is why the Earth God is especially popular with Hong Kong's shop owners, as every business can use a good security guard!

Sometimes seen accompanying the Earth God by the side of a doorway is the tablet of a higher god, who has his shrine set appropriately above that of the Earth God. This is Tin Kung, the Sky God, also known as the Fuk God of the Fuk-Luk-Sau trinity—the three household gods who respectively bless you with a life of bliss, plenty and longevity. Then, we have Choi Shen, the God of Wealth, whose extra importance to business entitles him to an elaborate indoor shrine. Finally, there is the increasingly popular Maneki Neko, the Japanese Beckoning Money Cat, which always sits facing the doorway, often near the cash register, and sometimes takes over the place of the Earth God.

Communal

In the past, an Earth God shrine was both an administrative marker and a spiritual totem set at the entrance to the smallest community unit, a cluster of 25 households, typically of the same clan, known as *she* (the Chinese term for "society" translates to mean "an assembly of *she*"). Today, communal Earth God shrines that serve as a marker and protector of settlements can still be found at almost every entrance to villages in Hong Kong's New Territories. These communal shrines, the size of a kitchen stove, were traditionally built of compacted earth and lime plaster. Today, they are built in brick and rendered with cement.[2]

Even though full-sized communal Earth God shrines are much less common in urbanised Hong Kong, where public spaces are carefully regulated and private spaces are at a premium, they can still be found in isolated laneways and backstreets in some of Hong Kong's oldest Chinese urban areas.[3] These areas, which are in today's Sheung Wan and Western Districts, include the Gage Street area,[4] the Nam Pak Hong area[5] and the Tai Ping Shan area.[6] Some of the shrines are urban remnants of past communities, while some were built after a catastrophic plague as added protection against future epidemics and the wandering ghosts of plague victims.[7]

Perhaps the most well-known of such shrines is the one built on a small platform, next to a flight of steps, at the junction of Peel Street and Staunton Street, the boundary area where Central District ends and Sheung Wan District begins. Despite its makeshift appearance, this shrine is endowed with official status that ensures its permanence. It is a modest place of worship registered with a grand name, the Pak Kung Temple (Pak Kung, or Grand Uncle, is another name for the Earth God), and it is managed by a statutory organization that carries a self-explanatory title, the Chinese Temples Committee. This explains why the shrine is well kept and well supplied with incense sticks and other offerings, despite the on-going urban renewal activities in the neighbourhood that are slowly bleeding out the old community.

At the dead end of Wo On Lane, within Central District's Lan Kwai Fong entertainment area, is a less well-known shrine. A freestanding miniature Chinese temple, it stands oblivious to the glare and din of bars, restaurants and fast-food joints in its surroundings. The shrine is named in honour of Fuk Tak, said to be a hardworking civil administrator who was posthumously deified as the Earth God.[8] Interestingly, for several years in the 1990s, before the drinking and dining crowds spread to Wo On Lane, the roof of this sturdy shrine was appropriated by a "street sleeper" (a homeless person in the Hong Kong nomenclature) as a liveable nest.[9]

Two even lesser known shrines, also named after the diligent Fuk Tak, can be found on Sheung Fung Lane and South Lane—obscure places whose names will draw blank faces among many Hongkongers. The former place is a stepped laneway in Sheung Wan District, one of Hong Kong's oldest Chinese urban settlements, while the latter is a back street in the Shek Tong Tsui area, infamously known in the early 20th century as Hong Kong's biggest legalized Chinese red-light district.[10] The commonality between both shrines is their incongruity and inconspicuousness within the setting of modern high-rise buildings. Like their counterparts on Peel Street and Wo On Lane, everyone agrees that the shrines are historical, but no one is sure about their exact vintage and the identity of the communities they once protected.

One cannot help but feel pity for these last surviving communal Earth God shrines. Every year, their relevance to the surrounding urban community diminishes as neighbourhoods undergo their cyclical renewal of people and buildings.

Transformation Instead of marking a community, most of today's urban shrines are associated with an individual business, usually a street-level shop, or a single household, frequently in an older apartment building. The prevalence of the Earth God shrine is revealed in a survey of a typical building in Wan Chai,[11] the 1963 May Wah Building (featured in another book by Michael Wolf, *Hong Kong Corner Houses*), which consists of seven shops on the ground floor and 84 home and home-business units on the twelve upper floors. All the ground-floor shops in this building have an Earth God shrine, and more than half of the upper-floor units have one as well.

Adapting to Hong Kong's congested urban environment means that the Earth God shrine is often represented by a small flat tablet and little else. This reduction in size allows it to compete for wall space with a host of modern utilities, including water pipes, sewage pipes, rainwater downpipes, air-conditioning unit drainpipes, water meters, electrical cables and fire-fighting water inlets. Sometimes, a tablet can be seen surrounded by shop signage, advertisement posters, graffiti or other visual clutter. When the opportunity arises, more territory is claimed for the Earth God by means of placing the tablet in a larger pre-fabricated tablet holder, or adding a space-claiming extension, such as an overhead canopy, a bigger cement pedestal and a sidewall made of cardboard, metal sheeting, plastic, plywood or any kind of handy material. Occasionally, a tablet is placed on a temporary pedestal made of found materials—loose bricks, cement blocks, floor tiles or even the lid of an old biscuit tin.

The transformation of the Earth God shrine mirrors the way people in urban Hong Kong frequently treat their living environment. Priority is given to practicality, while aesthetics is sometimes treated with indifference—whatever works, never mind how it looks, which, ironically, has produced a unique style that helps define Hong Kong.

Anatomy

The most basic and essential component of an Earth God shrine is a tablet representing the god. What are the tablets made of? What are they worth? To find out, the authors ventured into several Chinese joss-paper shops to investigate.[12] Perhaps, thanks to blessings from the Earth God, shop owners were surprisingly forgiving of our rummaging in their shops and tolerant of our torrent of questions.

But we were let down by the truth discovered. Far from the sacred religious object we thought it would be, the modern Earth God tablet is an astonishingly unsentimental mass-produced item—functional, dispensable, replaceable. The cheapest tablet, costing HK$5, is simply the god's name printed on a piece of paper mounted on fibreboard. For HK$18, his name is protected by a piece of glass mounted in a simulated gold frame, and this is the most common variety found by the doorway of shops along many Hong Kong streets. Paying more begets better materials, from veneered plywood costing tens of dollars to solid hardwood worth hundreds of dollars, a cost that renders such tablets suitable only for indoor installation.

Just as there is variety in tablet materials, there is also variety in its design. There are tablets made with an integrated lower tray, extended like the lower part of the letter "L," which provides a place for a small joss-stick urn. One possible accessory is the "god house." Looking like a cross between a bird house and a letterbox, built of wood (plywood or hardwood, depending on the price), it is essentially an open-face container that provides a shrine-like enclosure for the Earth God tablet.

While the space-saving tablet remains the most popular representation of the Earth God in urban Hong Kong, sometimes a different manifestation can be spotted: a porcelain figurine of a kind and happy-looking white-bearded old man, sitting and holding a staff in one hand. Like its tablet counterpart, this anthropomorphic representation of the Earth God comes in varying degrees of quality that correspond directly to the price tag. However, the larger and finer figurines are almost always kept in shrines installed indoors because of their cost and fragility.

A completely non-anthropomorphic representation of the Earth God comes in the form of a simple piece of natural stone, the size of which, dictated by precious space, can vary from the size of a potato to that of a pomelo. Such a representation is economical as well, as the stone can simply be found instead of paid for, perhaps picked up in the hills or from mountain streams. However, it cannot be just any stone, but a stone with certain qualities—it has to be egg-shaped and regular in form, texture and colour. Like figurines, stones representing the

Earth God remain rare in a big city, where spatial intrusion and conspicuousness may incur the hazard of mischievous theft, mindless vandalism or careless feet.

<table><tr><td>Consecration</td><td>

The Earth God's protection of shops and homes does not begin with the placing of a tablet, a figurine or a stone by the doorway. It begins with "activating" the object by inviting the Earth God to enter it. At first, we thought the consecration of a shrine would involve elaborate rituals performed by Taoist priests. We were again let down by our findings. The wife of a family-owned joss-paper shop in Wan Chai, who identified herself generically as "Mrs. Wong," explained matter-of-factly, "It's very simple, and you can do it yourself—and it's very cheap! Go to a flower stall in a street market and buy a branch of pomelo leaves, wet the branch with tap water, brush it on the tablet and it's done."[13] Of course, an auspicious date has to be chosen, to which Mrs. Wong said, "You can easily find an auspicious date by consulting the fortune calendar in the Tung Shing (the Chinese Almanac). Buy a copy from my shop—it's very cheap!"

</td></tr></table>

Not quite satisfied with a shorthand answer from a busy shop owner, we decided to interview seasoned practitioners of Earth God worship. However, we soon discovered that details of the consecration seemed to vary with every person interviewed. The truth is that in Chinese folk-religion practices, there really is no "correct" protocol as long as the essence is observed, and the details vary among individuals depending on family tradition. As one interviewee, Mrs. Shum, pointed out, "Some people might choose to do it in a quick and simple way, and I can't say it doesn't work, but I choose to do it the way it's been practised by my parents and grandparents."

After the invitation comes the welcoming: the newly arrived Earth God is offered three obligatory joss-sticks accompanied by the burning of joss-paper, as well as a special offering of meat and fruit and tiny cups of tea or wine. This welcoming feast for the god is repeated only on special occasions, usually during the Chinese New Year, while three burning joss-sticks suffice on ordinary days. The quality and quantity of the special offering are often a matter of generosity and sometimes expediency. For meat, it can range from a thin slice of roast pork to a cooked chicken and a whole roasted suckling pig. For fruit, the choice can vary from kumquats to oranges, apples, Chinese pears and tangerines, or a mixture of different kinds. Three is the nominal number, but limited space often results in exceptions: a lonely single, a contended pair or trio, a happy foursome or a full-house of five stacked in a pyramid. Pomelos, however, are always solitary, because of their ample size.

To celebrate the occasion, the Earth God tablet is decorated with two paper aigrettes, worn like two little horns on the head of the tablet, and draped with a bright red sash. No one seems to know anything about the significance of these decorations. When asked, the reply is unsatisfactorily hollow, "To show respect for the god, I suppose."

We had assumed that the ritual tradition of worshipping the gods would be as honoured as ancient sacred laws—stable, secure, unchanging. It therefore came as a surprise when we found out how casually the Earth God is treated today. Instead of being revered or feared, as gods should be, the Earth God is frequently ignored by his human host, much like an unloved household pet. In a survey of younger professionals in their 30s and 40s,[14] we found that the Earth God shrine is often an inconvenient inheritance from parents or grandparents. In many cases, the younger generation expressed a lack of interest in carrying on the tradition because they considered it too bothersome or because they had become Christians. Yet, while tradition fades away, empathy for the neglected Earth God lingers. In one case, when a pet dog peed on a roadside shrine, the dog's owner, a Christian, feared that she might have offended the Earth God and apologised profusely.[15]

Unsurprisingly, our survey revealed that those who carry on the tradition make daily offerings of incense, and special offerings of meat and fruit on festive occasions. For the less dedicated, disinterested or half-hearted, offerings to the Earth God are often scant and infrequent, the token three sticks of burning joss-sticks being the norm and offered at the convenience of the host. Some stopped the burning offering after becoming parents—their children's respiratory health taking precedence over the god's needs. In a 2011 court case, a protective new mother successfully sued her older neighbour for the latter's overly enthusiastic offering of burning joss-sticks to the Earth God shrine along the corridor.[16]

Perhaps the lack of respect for the Earth God is due to his lowly status in the rigidly hierarchical Chinese pantheon. A Chinese household is supposedly protected by "Nine Great Gods" (sometimes this divine protection squad is expanded to eleven or thirteen gods), each looking after a different aspect of the overall well-being of the household. When they are honoured in a home, their names and titles are prominently displayed in a framed glass plaque, above the names of the host's ancestors. The names of the gods are hierarchically arranged in the order of the Chinese court—the emperor occupying the centre and the ministers alternately positioned, with the most important to the emperor's left hand, the next most important to his right hand, and so on.[17]

The gods selected amongst the mighty nine vary, but Kwun Yam (also known as Guan Yin), the all-powerful Goddess of Mercy, is always the most revered household god and honoured with the central position. Other lesser gods are chosen depending on whether they are needed. For example, Pak Tai, God of the North Star, who controls water, is always welcome because of his prowess in preventing fire, one of the most dreaded household hazards. A family running a home business may include Kwan Tai (Guan Di), who is commonly referred to as the "God of War" in the West, which is a misnomer—the deified general is a god of honour, trust and loyalty, virtues important to people in business. Another family, whose members include a fisherman or sailor, may include Tin Hau, the protector of seafarers. Sometimes, the humble Earth God may not find a place among the Nine Great Gods. And when he does make it to be one of the nine, his name appears to the far right of Kwun Yam.

While honoured household gods rest on altars inside homes, the urban
Hong Kong Earth God is usually alone and outside the doorway, threatened by
pets and feet and frequently without the warmth of burning joss-sticks. And yet,
he is the most visible of the gods. His humbleness makes him the only god
we feel comfortable enough to call by such affectionate names as "Grandpa" and
"Grand Uncle." Like an elderly family member, we may have taken his presence
for granted, treating him with more tolerance than reverence.

Increasingly, there are signs that even our tolerance may be waning. Complaints
about incense fumes and intrusion into public space have driven the Earth God
inside homes and business premises, out of public sight. In Hong Kong's
public rental housing blocks, where 31% of the local population live,[18] rules that
forbid the placing of Earth God shrines outside doorways were once lax,
but are now strictly enforced.[19] The same restriction applies to many newer private
apartment blocks regulated by management companies. In many areas
that have undergone urban renewal, where small shops have given way to large
shopping malls and family businesses replaced by international franchises,
street shrines of the Earth God have largely disappeared. Walking along
Queen's Road Central, in the heart of Hong Kong's business district, we find very
few Earth God shrines remaining. In many ways, Hong Kong's Earth God is
very much like an older family member, whose presence will only be missed when
he is gone. This book is a timely tribute to a small god, losing ground, in a big city.

Readings

For a god whose shrines are ubiquitous along Hong Kong's crowded urban streets, there are curiously few published materials about him, especially in English. While the Internet seemingly carries much more information, careful browsing reveals that much of the information is the same material recycled among websites. Because of this literary limitation, as well as the authors' intention not to repeat what has already been written, this essay largely relies on primary material gathered from field research and interviews. For readers interested in finding out more about the historical or spiritual identity of the Earth God, and about the traditional shrines dedicated to him, here are some reading recommendations.

John H. Chamberlayne's article "The Chinese Earth-Shrine" (1966), provides detailed information about the folklore and tradition of the Hong Kong Earth God.[20] Hugh Baker's delightful book, *Ancestral Images: A Hong Kong Collection* (2011) contains an essay entitled "Earth God," which is about Earth God shrines in the New Territories.[21] A highly recommended Chinese publication is Carmen Wong Ka-man's *Daughter · Of God Painters* 王家敏《畫神像的 · 女兒》(2009), an informative and heart-warming autobiography of growing up with parents who ran a business painting pictures of gods and ancestral tablets.[22]

Wong's book, a winner of the second Young Writers' Competition in 2008, is preceded by her own dissertation submitted for the MSc (Conservation) Degree, "Painted Gods: Arts and Crafts for the Production of Ancestral Tablets and Folk Gods Plaques in Hong Kong" (2007).[23] A more recent dissertation for the same degree is Emma Law Ka-man's "Chinese Guardian Angel: A Study of the Changing Form of the Earth God (Tudi) from the Village to the City" (2010), in which she explains the Earth God tradition in rural and urban Hong Kong.[24]

Bibliography

Chamberlayne, John H. "The Chinese Earth-Shrine." In *Numen*, Vol. 13 (Oct. 1966), pp. 164–182.

Law, Ka-man Emma. "Chinese Guardian Angel: A Study of the Changing Form of the Earth God (Tudi) from the Village to the City." MSc (Conservation) dissertation, The University of Hong Kong, 2010.

Lee, Ho Yin and Lynne DiStefano. *A Tale of Two Villages: The Story of Changing Village Life in the New Territories.* Hong Kong: Oxford University Press, 2002.

Pryor, E. G. "The Great Plague of Hong Kong." In *Journal of the Hong Kong Branch of the Royal Asiatic Society*, Vol.15 (1975), pp. 61–70.

Wong, Ka-man Carmen. "Painted Gods: Arts and Crafts for the Production of Ancestral Tablets and Folk Gods Plaques in Hong Kong." MSc (Conservation) dissertation, The University of Hong Kong, 2007.

Wong, Ka-man Carmen. *Daughter · Of God Painters* 王家敏《畫神像的 · 女兒》. Hong Kong: Joint Publishing, 2009.

Acknowledgements

Sincere thanks to the students and alumni of The University of Hong Kong's Architectural Conservation Programmes (ACP) for their helpful cooperation in our Earth God survey. Special thanks to Katie Cummer for carrying out and coordinating the research for the essay, as well as for editorial input. We also would like to thank Sandy Shum Wai Yee for her assistance in the Chinese text and supplemental research. Additional thanks to Ng Yuk Hang for conducting the interviews with the Earth God shrine worshippers and custodians, recounted at the end of this book. Last but not least, our thanks to Michael Wolf, whose small comments made a big difference.

Notes

1. This phrase is Romanised in the Eitel/Dyer-Ball system adopted by the colonial administration of Hong Kong and in continued use by the Government of the Hong Kong Special Administrative Region.

2. Interestingly, traditional Chinese horseshoe graves in the New Territories have undergone similar modernisation, which makes one wonder if the shrine builders may have also been grave builders.

3. Hong Kong's traditional urban areas are located along the northern coastal strip of Hong Kong Island and the entire Kowloon Peninsula from Tsim Sha Tsui to Boundary Street. Urban development on Hong Kong Island began soon after the arrival of the British in 1841, while that of the Kowloon Peninsula began after its annexation by the British in 1860. The earliest Chinese urban settlements were confined to the north-western part of Hong Kong Island, roughly the areas west of Pottinger Street. For more information on Hong Kong's early Chinese settlements, see: Lee Ho Yin, "*Tong Lau*: A Hong Kong Shophouse Typology," a resource paper for the Antiquities and Monuments Office and the Commissioner for Heritage's Office, in the Hong Kong Collection of The University of Hong Kong (HKU) Main Library.

4. This is the area below Caine Road, between Pottinger Street and Aberdeen Street.

5. Nam Pak Hong ("North-South Trading Companies") is the area along Bonham Strand and Bonham Strand West. The name refers to companies that traded goods from the north (Mainland China) and the south (Southeast Asia). Until the establishment of the People's Republic of China in 1949, many of such companies were located along these two streets.

6. This is the area below Caine Road and above Queen's Road West, between Shing Wong Street and Po Yan Street.

7. In May 1894, a bubonic plague outbreak erupted in the City of Victoria and the epicenter of this catastrophic epidemic was Tai Ping Shan, the biggest Chinese settlement at the time. The severity of the outbreak is shown by the fatality statistics: from 1894 to 1901, the disease killed 95% of some 9,000 infected cases. See: E. G. Pryor, "The Great Plague of Hong Kong," *Journal of the Hong Kong Branch, Royal Asiatic Society*, Vol. 15 (1975): 64.

8. There are other accounts relating to the identity of Fuk Tak, but the hardworking civil administrator is the most common.

9. This was witnessed by one of the authors, Lee.

10. Shek Tong Tsui ("Stony Pond Beak," originally a granite quarry, hence the name) was a legalized Chinese red-light district from 1904 to 1935 and then from 1942 to 1945 during the Japanese Occupation of Hong Kong. For more information, see: Cheng Po Hung, *Early Prostitution in Hong Kong* (Hong Kong: Hong Kong University Museum and Art Gallery, 2010).

11. The field survey was carried out by Katie Cummer in November 2011.

12. The authors conducted the investigation in early March 2012, visiting a row of joss-paper shops on Queen's Road West, below Sai Ying Pun Jockey Club Polyclinic.

13. Although this "activation" process is common knowledge, the authors still sought verification from the operator of a flower stall at the Gage Street Market and received affirmation.

14. The survey was carried out in October 2011. A questionnaire was e-mailed to 295 students and graduates of the HKU Architectural Conservation Programmes; 45 responses were received.

15. The authors wish to thank Ms. Euphen Wong for this story.

16. This case was widely reported in the local media. See: Natalie Wong, "Curses caught on video in incense dustup at flats," *The Standard* (24 May 2011); Austin Chiu, "Injunction granted to curb incense-burning" and "Incensed woman wins HK$75,000 payout," *South China Morning Post* (4 June 2011).

17. Details of the Great Nine Gods can be found in Carmen Wong Ka-man's *Daughter · Of God Painters* 王家敏《畫神像的·女兒》(Hong Kong: Joint Publishing, 2009).

18. Percentage figure from the 2006 Population By-census Office, Census and Statistics Department, in Table E101, "Population by Type of Housing, 1996, 2001 and 2006."

19. The authors wish to thank Mr. Rick K. S. Lee, Architectural Services Department, and Ms. Rosman C. C. Wai, Hong Kong Housing Department, for confirming this information.

20. Chamberlayne's article is in *Numen*, Vol. 13 (Oct. 1966), pp. 164–182. It can be found online.

21. Baker's 2011 book is a compilation of essays from his three earlier books published by the South China Morning Post: *Ancestral Images: A Hong Kong Album* (1979); *More Ancestral Images: A Second Hong Kong Album* (1980); and *Ancestral Images Again: A Third Hong Kong Album* (1981). All of Baker's books are available at the HKU Main Library.

22. Wong's book is available at the HKU Fung Ping Shan Library and in the HKU Main Library's Hong Kong Collection.

23. Wong's dissertation can be found online through the HKU Scholars Hub's "Browse by Thesis Degree" website (search under: Master of Science in Conservation).

24. Law's dissertation can be found online through the HKU Scholars Hub's "Browse by Thesis Degree" website (search under: Master of Science in Conservation).

繁華都市小小神
香港市區中的土地神位

英文原作: 李浩然 Lee Ho Yin
　　　　　狄麗玲 Lynne D. DiStefano
中文譯文: 李浩然 Lee Ho Yin
　　　　　岑慧儀 Sandy Shum Wai Yee

土地財神　一個鄉下小神駕臨繁華大都會，會有甚麼遭遇呢？我們原本以為攝影師吳爾夫（Michael Wolf）是以這樣的想法來拍攝這一輯土地神位的照片。他知道後，馬上跑來澄清：「我不是拍土地神位的寫真集！我拍的是神位周圍的情況，是都市人怎麼用盡法子把神位塞入鬧市的環境！」因此，我們重新構思，把文章集中在土地神的風俗是如何融入現今城市化的香港社會。

如果你問：土地神是誰？你只會得到一連串的傳說典故。其實要真正了解土地神，你應該問：土地神是甚麼？今天我們在香港市區中所看到的土地神，很多時候是用一塊寫上「門口土地財神」的簡單神牌所代表。可能是財迷心竅之故，人們看到「財神」兩字，就忘記了「土地」，把兩個不同的神混為一體。其實，以往農民的財富是來自土地的耕種，所以土地亦是財神。

事實上，土地是一位守財之神，而不是運財之神。所以在香港這個商業城市，開店做生意的特別喜歡供奉土地神，試問有誰不想有神靈來保護辛辛苦苦賺來的錢啊！有時候，我們可以看到土地神位之上還有一個天官的神位，反映著後者更高的神階。除了福神天官，我們還有更受商戶歡迎的財神爺，他的神位一般被供奉在室內，反映著他在商戶心目中的地位。還有，通常擺放在收銀處的東洋招財貓亦愈來愈流行，有時候會看到神敵不過貓的情況，原本應該擺設土地神位的位置被招財貓霸佔了。

福德神社　在春秋戰國時代，供奉土地的神社是一個戶籍制度的標誌，代表著二十五戶人口為一「社」。到了今天，戶籍制度已不同了，但保祐整個社區的土地神社，我們仍然可以在香港新界各鄉村的入口處看到。在寸金尺土與規例繁多的香港市區裡，這些有如灶頭般大的神社已十分罕見。然而，少數的神社仍然隱藏在上環與西環的橫街窄巷中，靜靜地等待著我們的偶遇。

在十九世紀中期，當香港島被英國人開發成為商業城市時，從內陸遷移到香港的華人大多數聚居在上環與西環的結志街、南北行、太平山等一帶，形成了香港早期的華人社區。[1] 這些鬧市中的土地神社，有些是歷史遺跡，有些是十九世紀末的太平山大瘟疫後設立的，用以保祐居民不再受災，免受冤魂滋擾。[2]
這些神社雖然為數不多，但亦不難找到。在上環卑利街和士丹頓街交界處就有
一個香火鼎盛的神社。這神社設在一排階梯旁的小平台上，看似簡陋，有點
像是臨時搭建的。雖有稍嫌誇大的「伯公廟」名堂，但該地方亦有政府註冊，
並由「華人廟宇委員會」這個法定組織看管。因此，就算社區陸續重建，拜神的
老街坊已日漸少見，該神社依然香火不斷。

另一個鮮為人知的神社，位於燈紅酒綠的蘭桂坊附近之安和里，像與世無爭
的隱士般靜靜地藏在橫街的盡頭。這座簡簡單單的神社，外形如一間袖珍小廟，
名字亦是實實在在的「福德祠」。在上世紀九十年代，一名街頭露宿者曾經佔用
神社的屋頂為他的臨時安樂窩。[3] 為什麼土地神經常與「福德」掛鈎呢？這有多方
面的說法，最普遍的說法是指一位名叫「福德」的父母官，生前刻苦耐勞，死後
被追封為神。石塘咀在二十世紀初曾是香港最大的合法華人紅燈區，[4] 當中
有一個更鮮為人知的土地神社。祂就位於南里，在周圍巨大的商場和高層
住宅群的蔭庇下，這座神社更顯孤立。和以上所述的神社一樣，它們的歷史意義
毋庸置疑，但它們原本所歸屬的社區已經不存在了，無從稽考。隨着舊社區歷年
來的更新與人口變化，這些僅餘的公共土地神社已逐漸式微，令人惋惜。

解剖神牌　　如今在香港市區公共地方供奉的土地神位，通常是簡簡單單的一個神牌。
這些土地神位並不保祐社群，而是歸屬個別家戶，而正如吳爾夫所説，它們隨處
可見。我們的研究員康嘉玲（Katie Cummer）在灣仔一座一九六三年建造的
美華大廈作了調查，發現這座大廈所有的七個地舖都設有土地神位，而樓上
十二層八十四家商住單位超過半數亦設有土地神位。（香港大學出版社於
二零一一年為吳爾夫出版的《街頭街尾》攝影集亦有提及此大廈。）

鑑於香港市區地少人多，土地神位亦有需要簡化為一塊佔地極少的神牌。只有
這樣的改變才可以令土地神能擠身於數之不盡的各式各樣的水管、水錶、
電線、電錶、消防喉等現代化設施中。有時候，土地神位還要浮沉於商店招牌、
廣告海報、塗鴉或其他視覺污染中。然而，人們總會把握一切機會給他們
供奉的土地神拓展更多的空間，比如給神牌加置神龕、建造遮蓋、加大基座等。
偶然會見到有些神位臨時設置在碎磚瓦上，甚至月餅盒中，似乎正在等候良機，
祈求在未來爭取一席之位。這些土地神位千變萬化地遷就它們的棲身之處，
正正反映了香港人怎樣無視美觀，務求實際。正因如此，這種務實的生活方式
也令香港城市別樹一格，產生了「香港式」的獨有風格。

看起來簡簡單單的土地神牌又到底有何乾坤呢？為了從中了解，兩位作者
走訪了位於皇后大道西的紙紮舖。[5] 可能是得到了土地神的保祐，店主和店員們
都在百忙中抽空回答我們不勝其煩的查詢。然而，所得的答案卻出乎我們的意料
之外，一直以為是聖物的神牌原來只是件凡俗的商品！花五港元就可以買到一塊
在纖維板上貼紙的神牌。而花十八港元換來的神牌就是最常見、有玻璃框的
那一種。俗語説：一分錢一分貨，土地神牌又何嘗不是？由幾十塊錢的夾板
到數百元的實木貨色都有，豐儉由人，任君選擇。有些神牌會整合香爐位或神龕，
設計上五花八門，價錢當然也不一樣啦！

雖然香港市區中絕大多數的土地神位都是些扁平的神牌，偶然也會遇到一些
立體的陶瓷土地公神像。它們的造形是一個坐得四平八穩，手持拐杖，面目慈祥，
帶着微笑的銀鬚老人。和神牌一樣，這種神像的價錢有別，地位也不一樣，
較為精緻和昂貴的神像一般都安置於室內的神龕裡。土地神亦可以用一塊天然
的石頭代替。石頭的大小可以小到像一個馬鈴薯，亦可以大如一個沙田柚。
這種表達土地神的方式也很經濟實惠，因為石頭不用花錢而隨處可得，可以
在登高遠足時順路撿獲，或在溪中撈起。但可以用來代表土地神的石頭是有
標準的，它的外形必須有如雞蛋般橢圓，表面與顏色亦要均勻。以神像或石頭
造形的土地神並不多見於鬧市中，因為稍為佔了行人通道或外形比較觸目的
物件，都可能惹來偷竊、惡意破壞、或慘遭八字脚橫掃的無妄之災。

安設土地神位的首要任務是迎接土地神上位。起初我們以為這個莊嚴的禮儀是需
要道士主持的。而事實又再一次讓我們感到意外。紙紮舖的老闆娘輕描淡寫地用
廣東話說：「咁好簡單啫！你自己去街市花檔買束碌柚葉（好平㗎！），用水喉水
濕濕佢，跟住掃吓個神牌，咁就搞掂㗎啦！」當然，請神上位必須要擇吉日，
老闆娘又說：「買本通勝自己查吓咪得囉！」我們當然有點懷疑，這麼神聖的
事情怎麼可以如此簡單？於是我們又走訪了一些拜土地神的人，發現原來上位
儀式各家各法，各廟各菩薩：有較為隨意，喜歡一切從簡的，亦有較為傳統，
堅持上一輩所承傳的。

土地神上位後，當然少不了來拜祭一番。除了例行的三炷香外，同時還需紙錢、
肉類、水果和茶酒等貢品。平日一般的拜祭，上三炷香就可以了。在農曆新年等重
要日子，用貢品拜神是免不了的，但貢品的質和量很多時候取決於供奉者的誠心
與方便。貢肉可以是一大塊燒肉、一隻熟雞或一整隻燒乳豬。貢果可以是橙、柑、
蘋果、雪梨等，數量上通常是三個，但是如果空間有限，有時寒酸得只有一兩個。
如地方容許，會見到像疊羅漢般擺放的四五個貢果。如果是體型較大的柚子，
通常只能擺放一個。[6]

在神位開光或時節等大日子，神位都會用簪花掛紅裝飾一番。「簪花」又名
「金花」，是金色紙造的頭簪，而「掛紅」是指中間有金球形狀裝飾物的掛身
紅布帶。當我們查詢這些飾物的含義時，一般的解釋都是尊敬神靈，似乎無人
可給予具體的答案。

<table>
<tr><td>土地不容</td><td>原本以為拜土地神是由古至今神聖不可侵犯的傳統。我們的調查又有出乎意料的
發現。面對法力無邊的神靈，凡人本應又敬又畏。現實上，現代城市人對待
土地神的態度是比較隨意的。在我們的問卷調查中（對象是香港大學建築文物
保護課程的畢業生，大多數是三四十歲的專業人士），[7]大部分人覺得住家門外
的土地神位是上一代傳下來的麻煩東西。對年青的一代來說，這不難理解。除了
沒興趣，嫌麻煩以外，有些人已成為基督徒，不可以拜神。然而，有一個有趣
的例子顯示到有些現代的城市人對土地神還留有敬畏。話說有一人，有一天帶着
寵物散步時，忽然發覺愛犬正在路旁一個被遺棄的土地神位撒尿。雖然該人是
基督徒，但仍然慌忙給淋了一頭狗尿的土地神鞠躬道歉！[8]</td></tr>
</table>

那些誠心供奉土地神的人，當然會天天上香，節日時拜神，而那些勉為其難承接
傳統的人，就沒有那麼虔誠了。我們的調查顯示，上香會變得不定時，
還要看心情，有些母親懷孕後，準父母為了胎兒的安危，乾脆連香也不上了。
在二零一一年就有這麼一則新聞：一位老婆婆屢屢在走廊為土地神位進香，
結果惹上官非，被初為人母的鄰居控告她過度燒香，影响了新生嬰兒的健康。[9]

近年來，都市人與土地神的相處漸見不容。為了避免面對燒香拜神的投訴，
不少供奉土地神的人都把土地神位從門外移到室內。有三成香港人口居住的
租用公共房屋，雖然沒有明文規定不可以在門口外安放神位，燒香拜神，
但隨着人們愈來愈懂得維護個人權益，以往在走廊通道中拜祭土地的習俗，
現今在佔用公共地方和滋擾左鄰右里的投訴下，變得難以持續。在專業物業管理
的新建私人大廈就更不用說了，大廈公契甚至明例禁止在公共地方擺設神位及
進行拜神等活動。[10]

諸神之中，為什麼土地神好像特別不受人敬畏呢？這可能與他的卑微地位有關。
傳統上，各戶人家有「九大神」(有時甚至是十一或十三大神）的保祐。
諸神的名銜被註在玻璃框架內的牌匾，排列在祖先名字之上。排列次序以中間
為主，先左後右。上榜的神要視乎他們的神通是否配合個別家戶所需。法力
無邊的觀音當然榜上有名，而且必定首排中位。能治水火之患的北帝，家戶常備。
講信用有義氣的關公，做生意的特別喜愛。能護航渡海的天后，靠海為生的
就少不了。而好像沒有甚麼法力的土地神，經常會榜上無名，只有留守在門口外。
就算有幸上榜的話，通常都被排到遠離觀音娘娘的極右之位。[11]

當尊貴的諸神安然置放在家居神枱上，受到香火鼎盛的待遇時，可憐的
土地神卻失落於繁華的香港大都會，面對人間冷暖，蒙受狗隻便溺之辱。然而，
在滿天神佛的鬧市凡間，土地神的曝光率還是名列前茅的。況且，凡人對他
最有親切感，被冠予「公公」、「爺爺」、「伯伯」等稱號。但是，也是因為這份
凡俗的親切感，他亦有時好像老人家般受到冷漠的對待。

今天當我們走入被重建的社區內，眼見的盡是「無神」的國際連鎖店與
大型商場，以前門口外設有土地神位的店舖已被淘汰了。同樣地，走上繁華的
皇后大道中，行人道上的土地神位簡直是鳳毛麟角，難以覓尋。可能有一天，
當我們猛然發現土地神已經在市區內消逝時，我們才會懷念他老人家曾經的
存在，依依不捨與他共渡的日子。

讀本好書　　話説回來，香港的土地神位好像隨街可見，但奇怪的是，有關的書籍和文章卻
少之又少。而在資訊氾濫的互聯網絡上找到的，其實是重複又重複的籠統材料。
所以本文的作者們只好揮着汗水，踏破鐵鞋，去尋找第一手鮮為人知而又有趣的
資料來撰寫這篇文章。

幸而，好的著作還是有的，中文書籍首選有王家敏的《畫神像的‧女兒》
（三聯書店，二零零九年出版）。此書是二零零八年第二屆年輕作家創作比賽
的獲獎作品，講述作者在一個製作神像與神主牌的家庭中成長的經歷。
王家敏是香港大學建築文物保護課程的碩士畢業生，她的畢業論文（二零零七年）
就是以親身的體驗詳細記錄了神牌的製作。而她的師妹羅嘉雯的碩士論文
（二零一零年），則把研究議題集中在香港鄉村與市區的土地神位之別。

英文著作方面有本地著名中國通教授裴達禮（Hugh Baker）的 *Ancestral Images:
A Hong Kong Collection*（香港大學出版社，二零一一年出版）。最後，大家不妨上
網搜索 John H. Chamberlayne 於一九六六年撰寫的一篇有關香港新界土地神社的
文章："The Chinese Earth-Shrine"。

致謝　　這篇文章的原文是用英文寫的，原本以為把原文直接翻譯成中文就行了，結果
是完全行不通，只好硬着頭皮依照原文的大意重新再寫。幸好有認識了二十多年的
老朋友岑慧儀小姐的協助，這份苦差才變得較容易，藉此向她深表感謝。同時，
我們亦感激黎志邦先生、孫莞瑤小姐和張捷飛先生為此文作出的努力。另特別致
謝伍育行小姐對本書後面的採訪部分所作出的貢獻。

註釋

1　　有關香港十九世紀的早期華人社區的中文著作為數不少，尤其是專門研究本地史的丁新豹、高添強、
鄭寶鴻、蕭國健等人的著作。

2　　有關香港十九世紀太平山瘟疫的中文著作，較近期的有香港三聯書店出版的《街角‧人情：香港砵甸乍街
以西》(2010)。根據記載，1894年由太平山爆發的瘟疫，感染者有九千多人，死亡率高達九成半，直到
1929年才平息。

3　　作者李浩然親眼所見。

4　　有關石塘咀紅燈區的歷史，最詳盡的記載有鄭寶鴻的中英雙語著作：《香江風月 Early Prostitution
in Hong Kong》（香港：香港大學美術博物館，2010）。

5　　作者李浩然和狄麗玲於2012年3月走訪了這些位於「西營盤賽馬會普通科門診診所」下面的紙紮舖。

6　　感謝岑家李蓉女士提供資料。

7　　此問卷調查是於2011年10月以電郵方式進行的。

8　　感謝黃若葦女士提供此故事。

9　　此「美孚荔灣花園女住客申請禁制鄰居燒香案」於2011年5月21日與24日以及同年6月4日與6日在香港
多份中文報章報導。

10　　感謝建築署的李金成先生與房屋署的衛翠芷女士提供資料。

11　　資料來源：王家敏，《畫神像的‧女兒》（香港：三聯書店，2009）。

Anatomy of an Earth God Shrine

The three forms of Earth God representation: **1** tablet; **2** figurine; **3** stone.

Decorations for the Earth God shrine: **4** red sash; **5** paper aigrettes (those with peacock feathers are for a god's shrine, and those without are for ancestors).

Accessories for the Earth God shrine: **6** joss-stick urn (the common sheet-metal type illustrated) with three joss-sticks and two candles; **7** "god house" (optional, depending on space available).

土地神位構造圖

三種代表土地神的物體：**1** 神牌；**2** 神像；**3** 石頭。

土地神位的裝飾品：**4** 掛紅；**5** 簪花 (有孔雀羽毛的簪花是拜神專用的，沒有孔雀羽毛的是拜祖先用的)。

土地神位的配件：**6** 插有三炷香與一對燭的香爐 (用鐵皮製造的香爐最為普遍)；**7** 神龕 (要視乎設置神位的地方是否有足夠空間容納)。

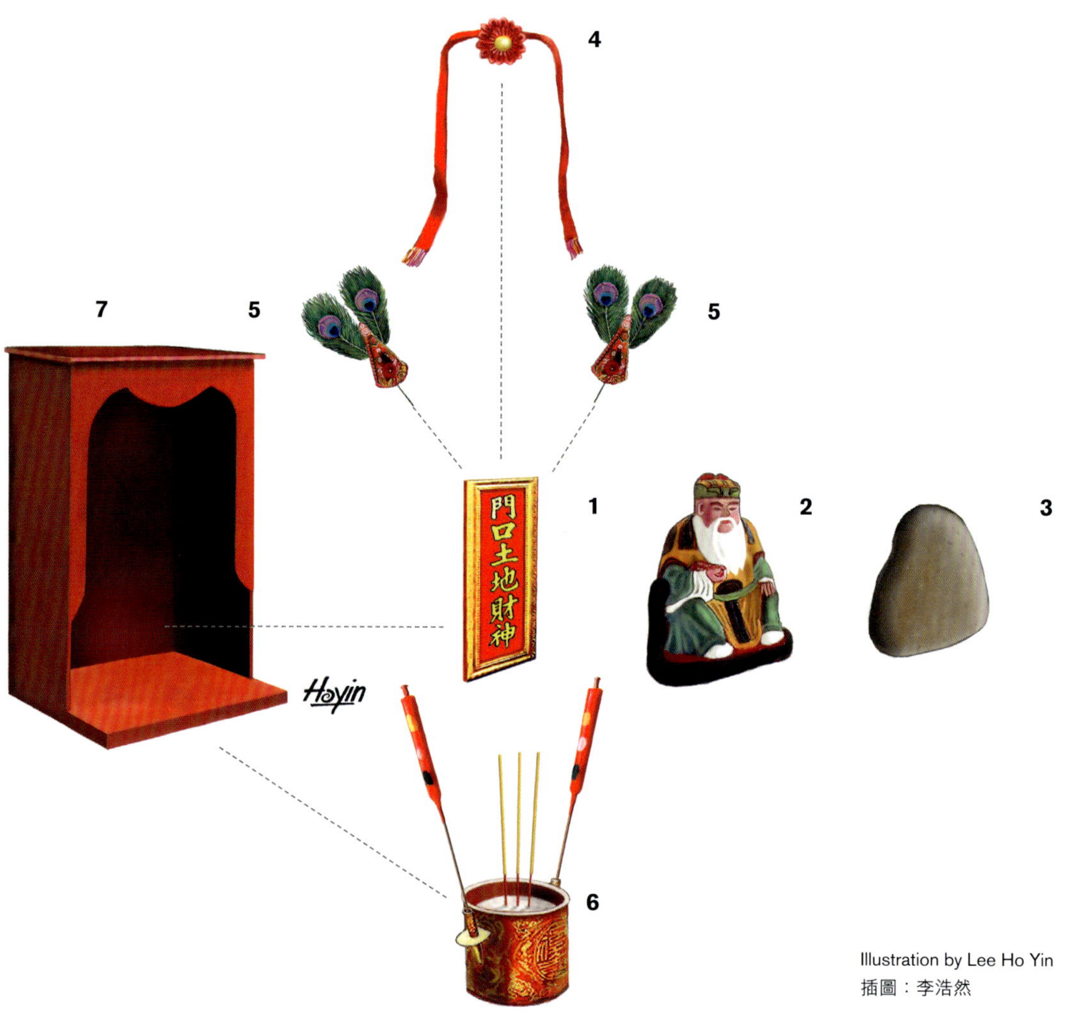

Illustration by Lee Ho Yin
插圖：李浩然

Earth God Shrines
Plates

土地神位
照片

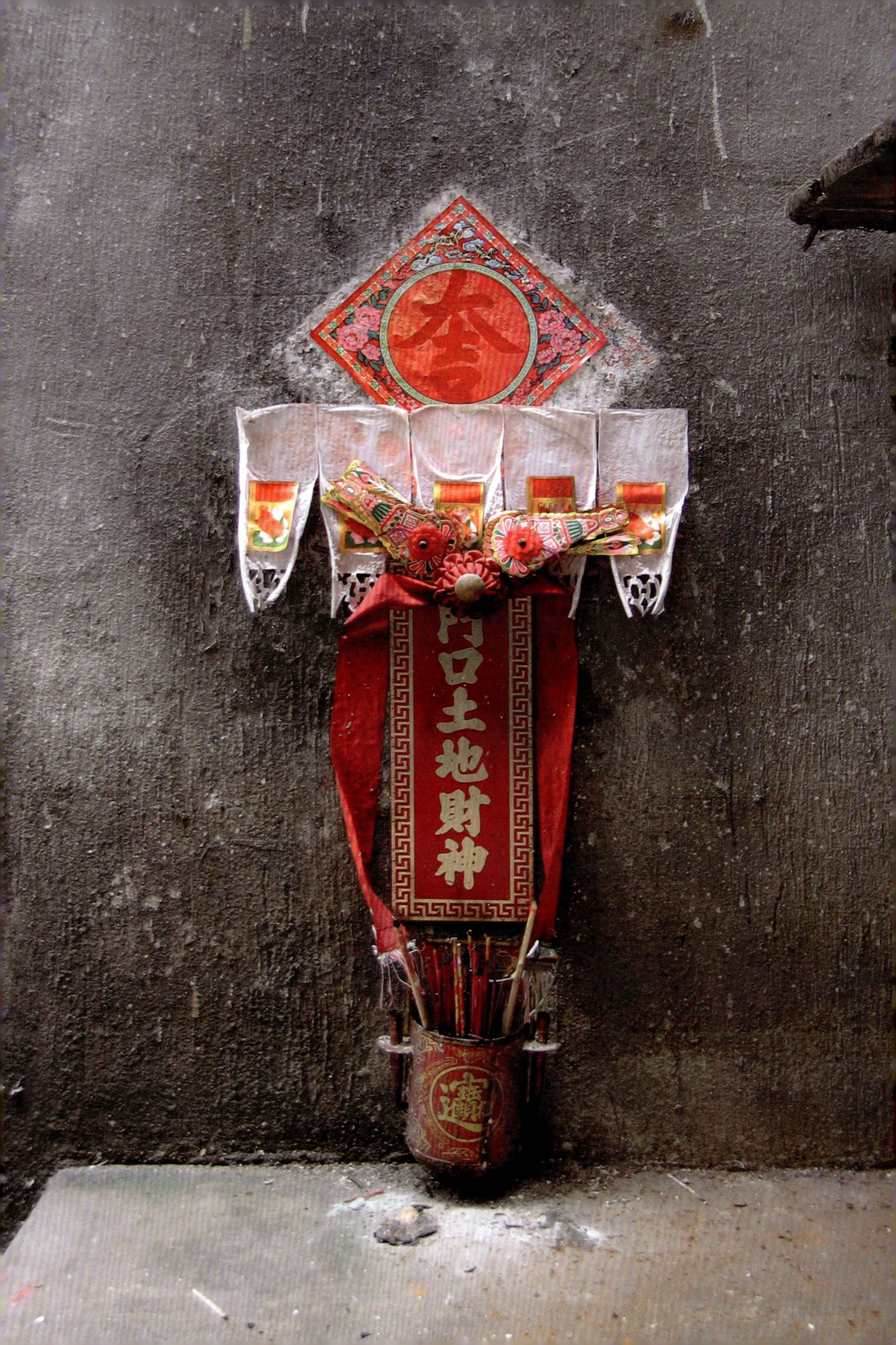

令
門口土地財神

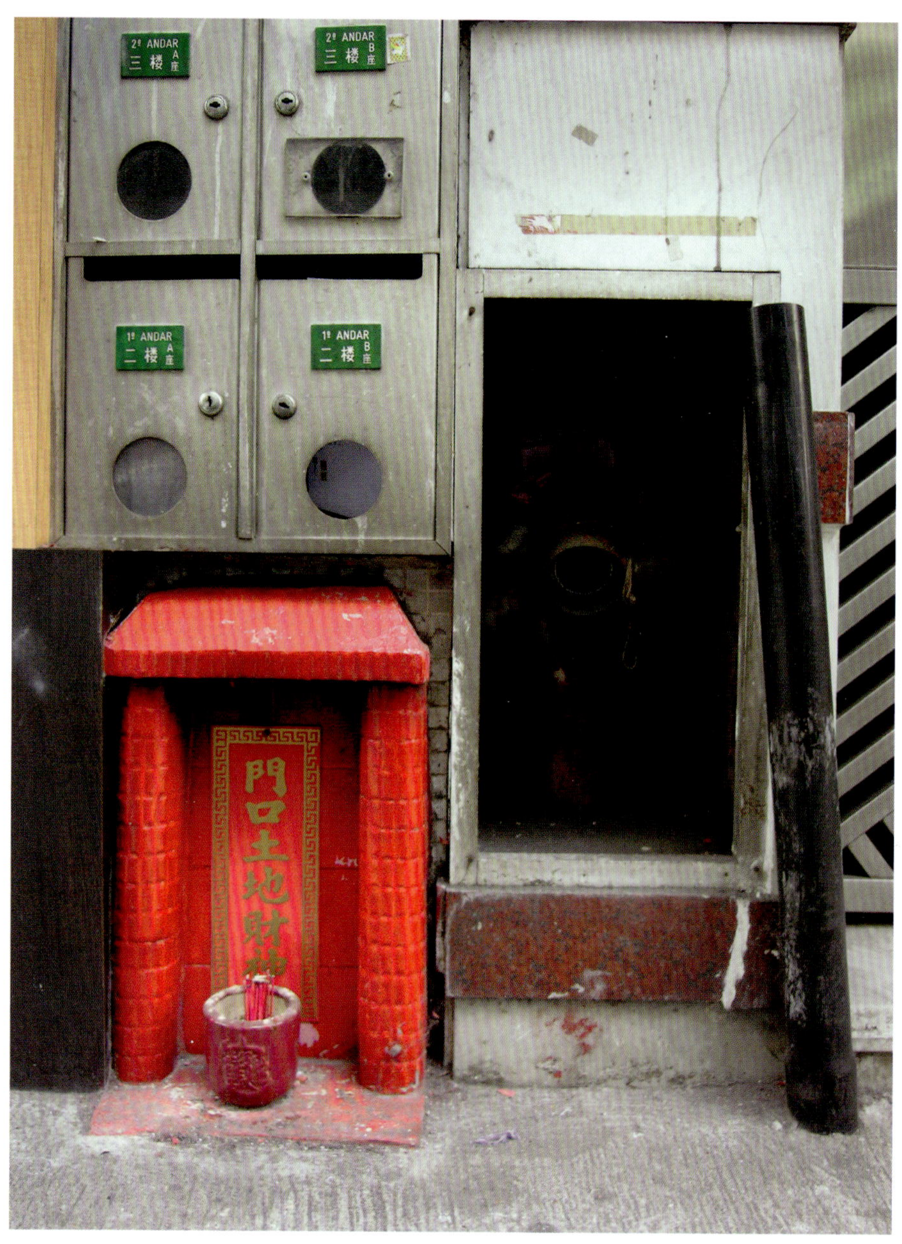
2º ANDAR
三樓 A座
2º ANDAR
三樓 B座
1º ANDAR
二樓 A座
1º ANDAR
二樓 B座
門口土地財神

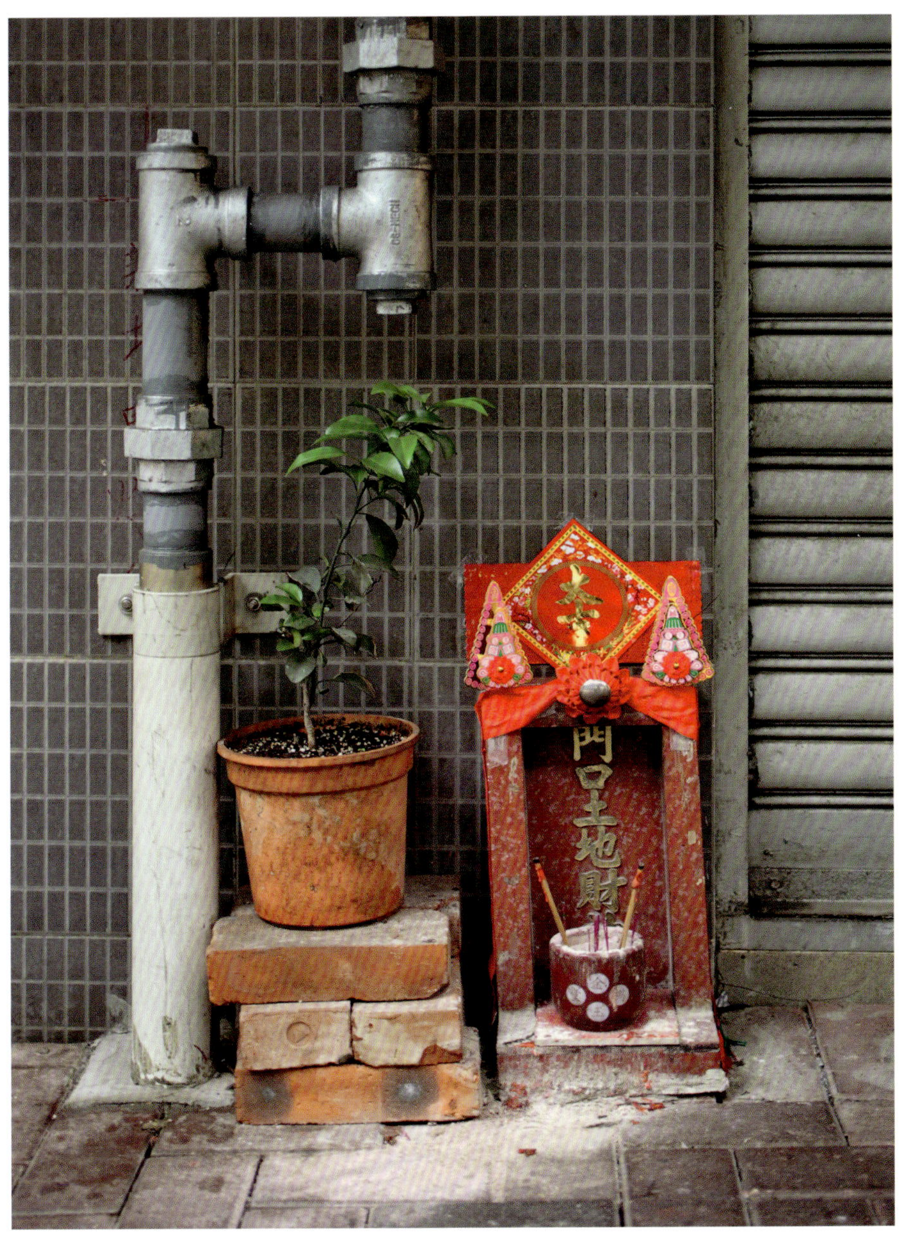

門口土地財

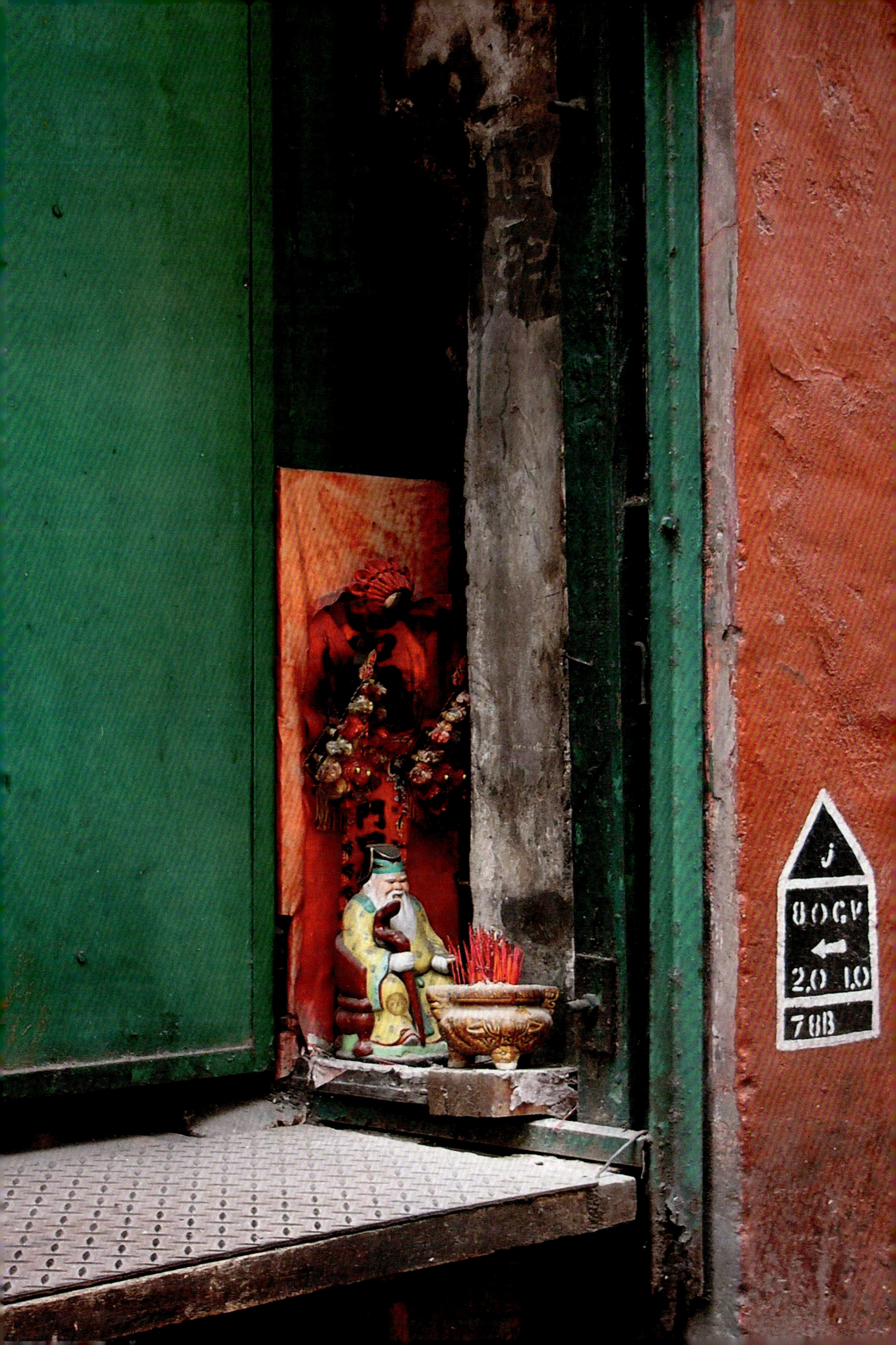
j
80GV
2.0 1.0
788

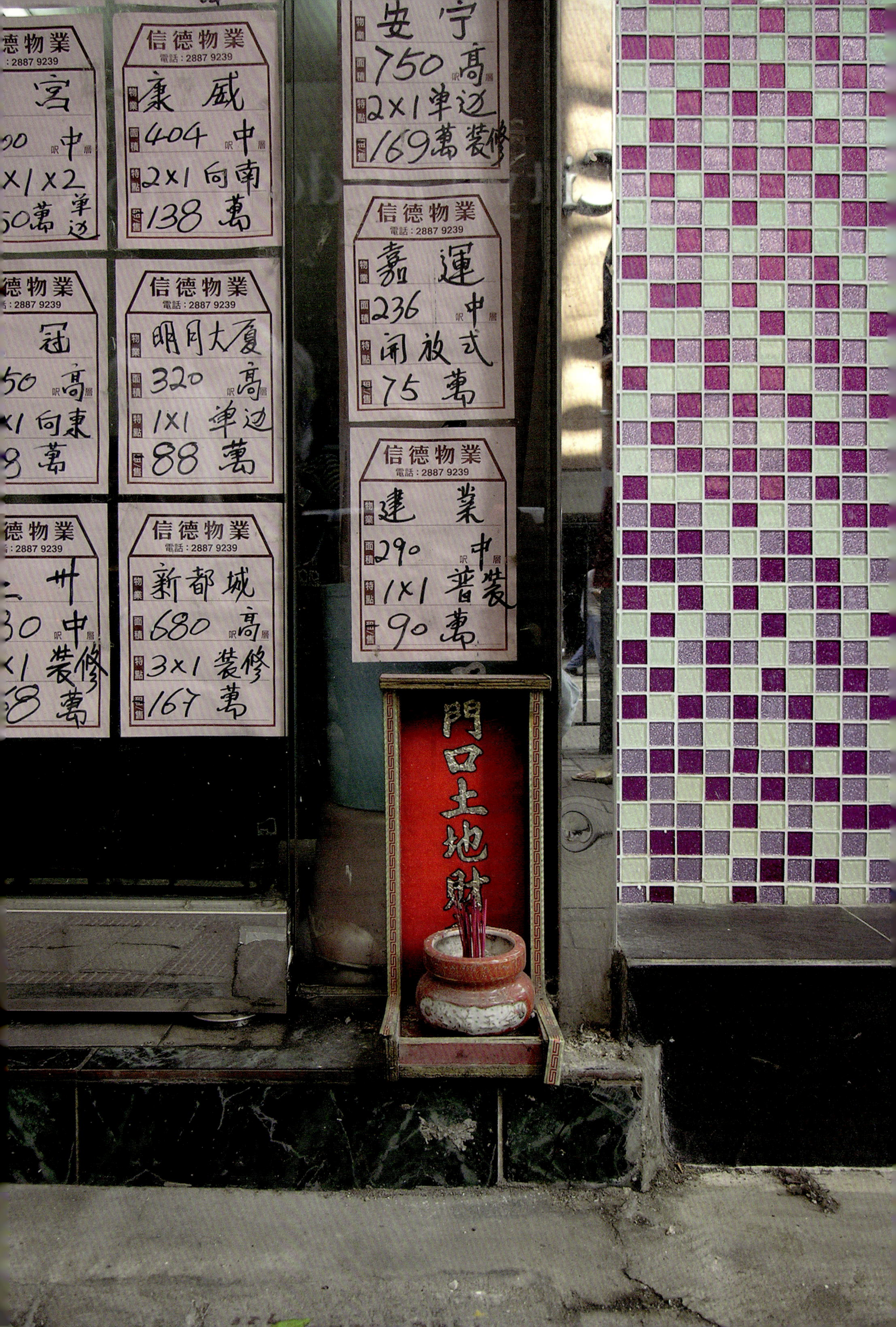
信德物業
電話: 2887 9239
宮
中
X1X2
萬
單边
信德物業
電話: 2887 9239
康 威
404 中
2X1 向南
138 萬
信德物業
電話: 2887 9239
冠
高
X1 向東
萬
信德物業
電話: 2887 9239
明月大廈
320 高
1X1 單边
88 萬
信德物業
電話: 2887 9239
中
30 中
X1 裝修
萬
信德物業
電話: 2887 9239
新都城
680 高
3X1 裝修
167 萬
安 宁
750 高
2X1 單边
169萬裝修
信德物業
電話: 2887 9239
嘉 運
236 中
開 放 式
75 萬
信德物業
電話: 2887 9239
建 業
290 中
1X1 普裝
90 萬
門口土地財

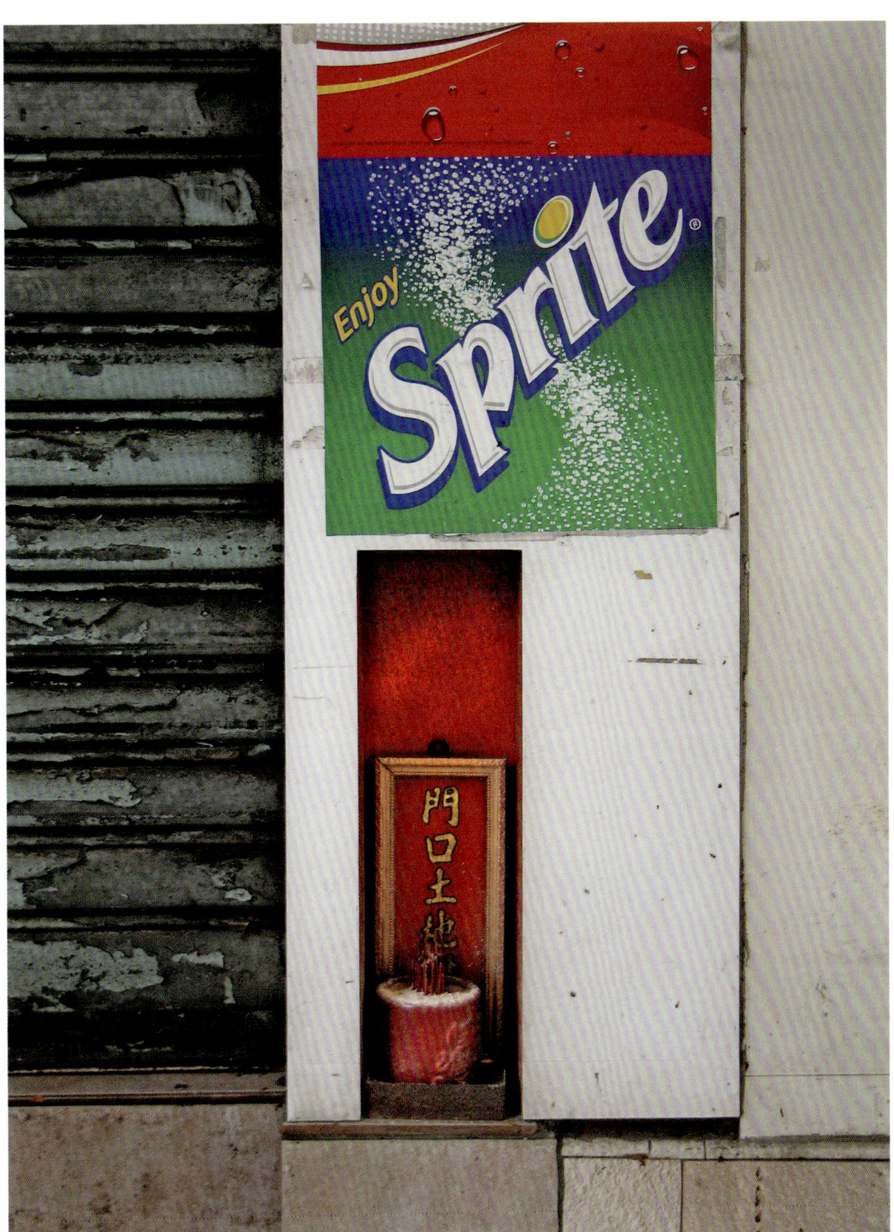

Enjoy
Sprite
門口土地

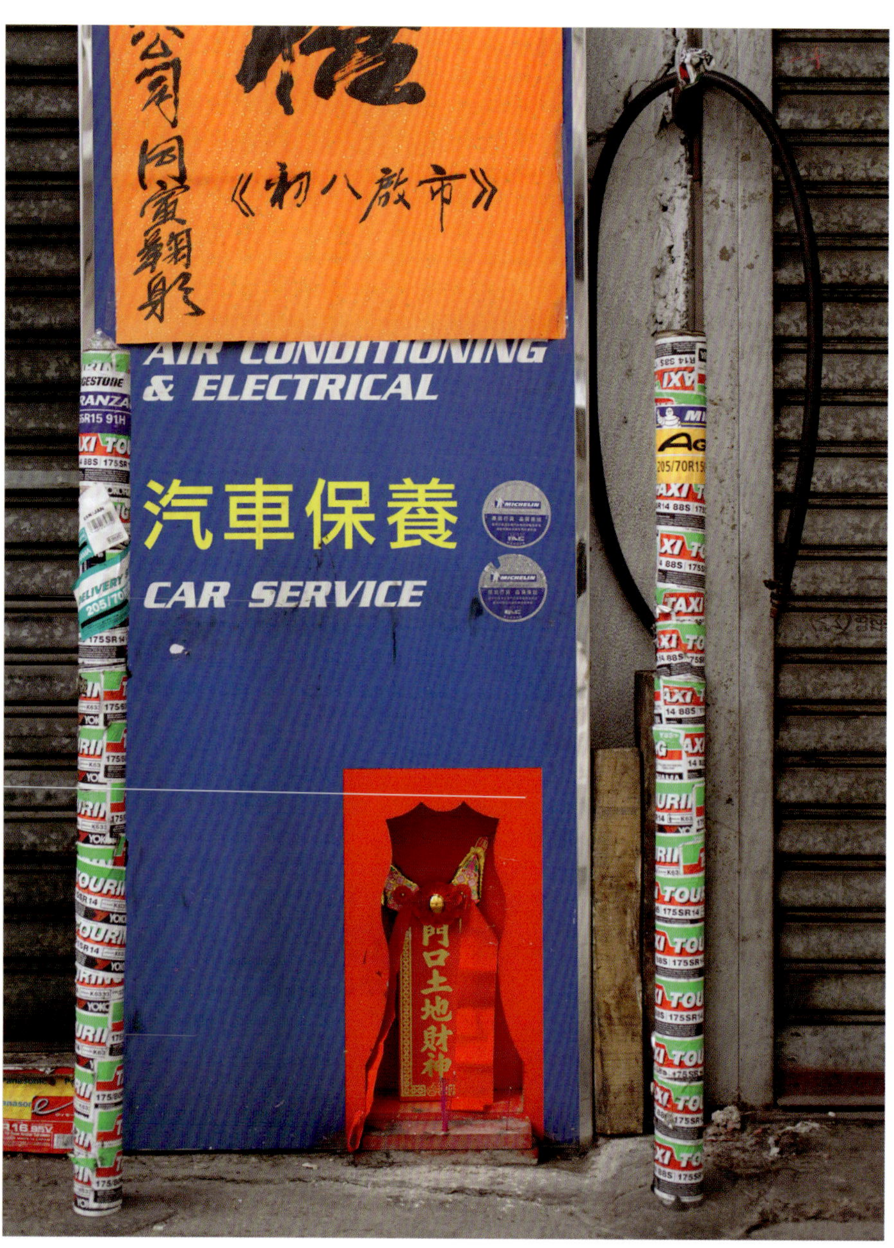
公司
同業翻影
《初八啟市》
AIR CONDITIONING
& ELECTRICAL
汽車保養
CAR SERVICE
門口土地財神

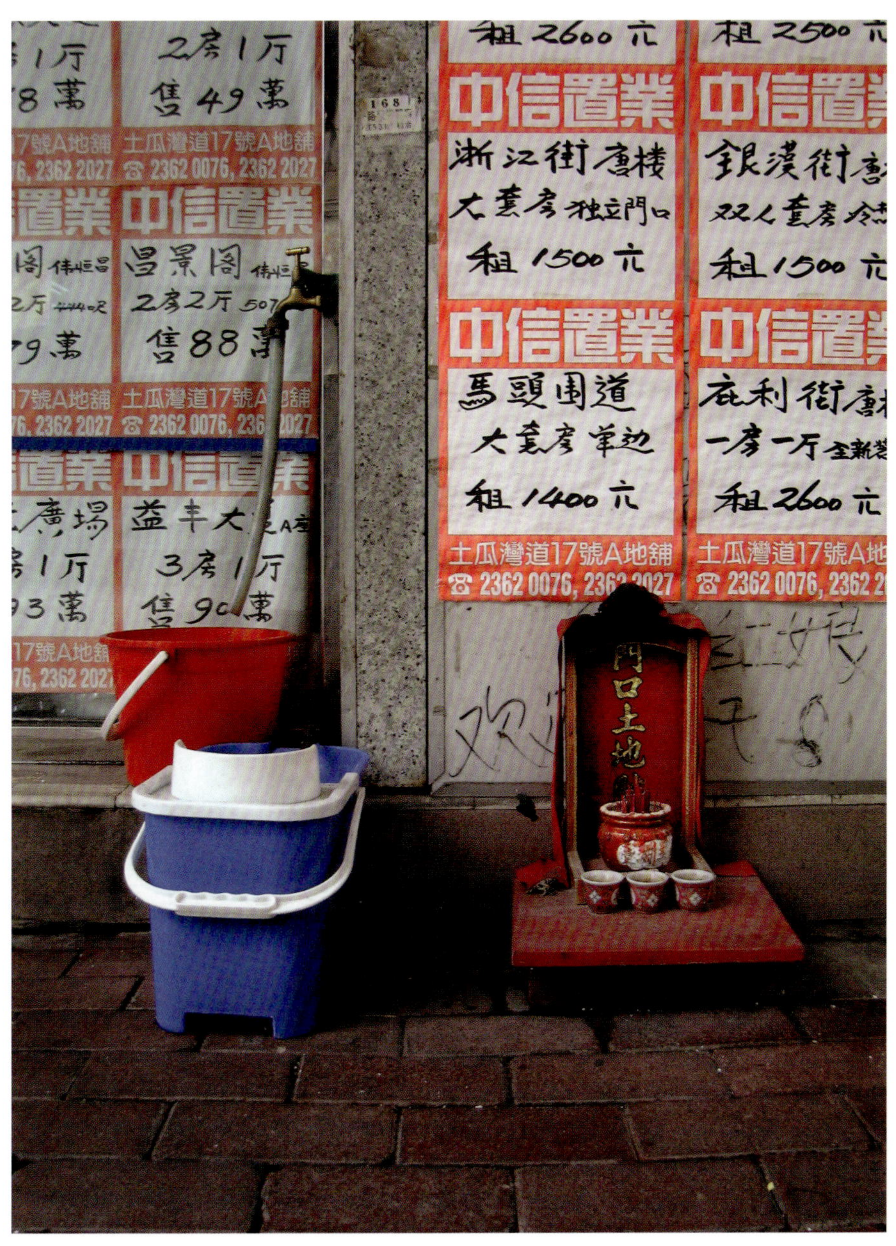
租 2600 元
租 2500 元
2房 1厅
售 49 萬
中信置業
中信置業
17號A地舖
土瓜灣道17號A地舖
浙江街唐樓
銀漢街唐
0076, 2362 2027
2362 0076, 2362 2027
大套房独立門口
双人套房
置業
中信置業
租 1500 元
租 1500 元
昌景閣
2房2厅
中信置業
中信置業
售 88
馬頭围道
在利街唐
17號A地舖
土瓜灣道17號A地舖
大套房革边
一房一万全新
0076, 2362 2027
租 1400 元
租 2600 元
置業
中信置業
土瓜灣道17號A地舖
土瓜灣道17號A地舖
廣場
益丰大
☎ 2362 0076, 2362 2027
☎ 2362 0076, 2362
房1厅
3房1厅
售 90 萬
17號A地舖
門口土地
0076, 2362 2027
168

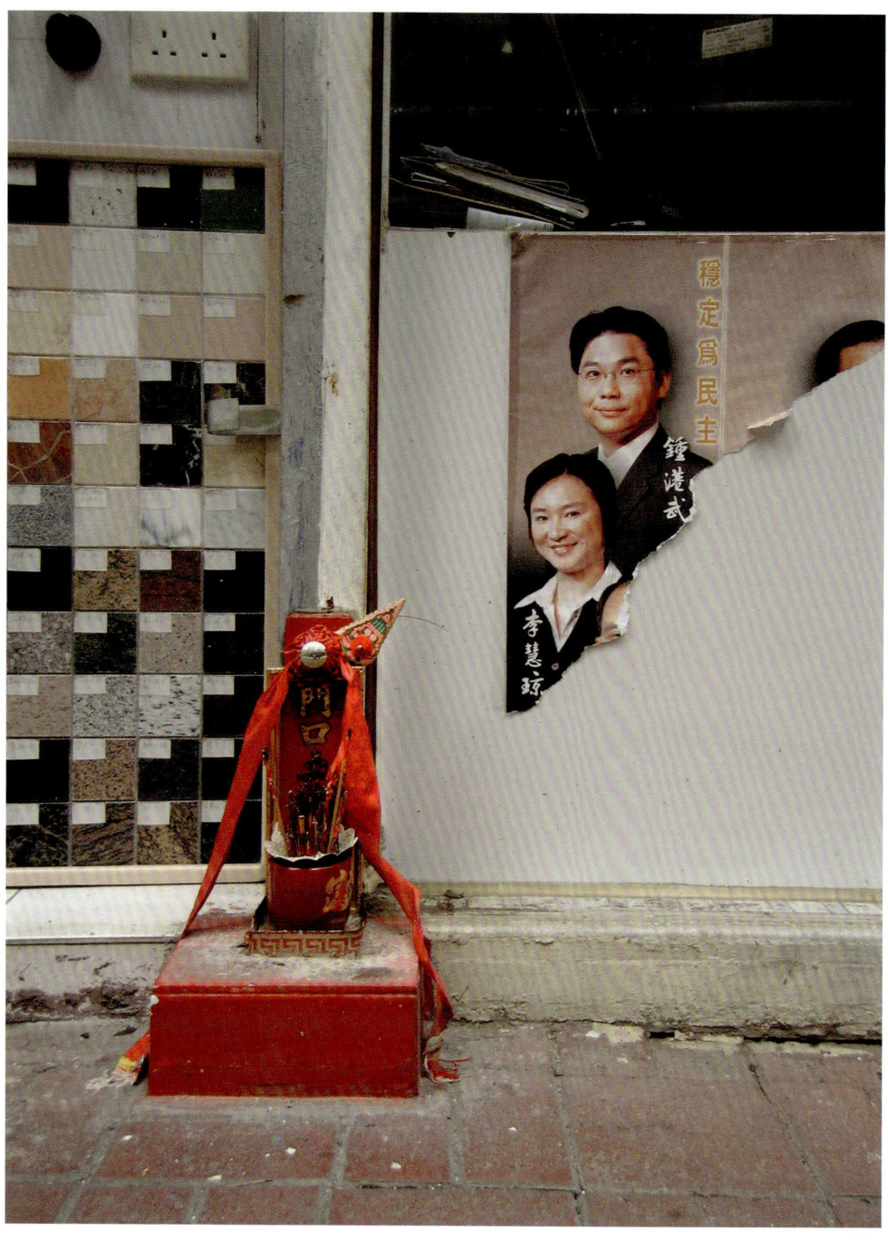
穩定為民主
鍾港武
李慧琼

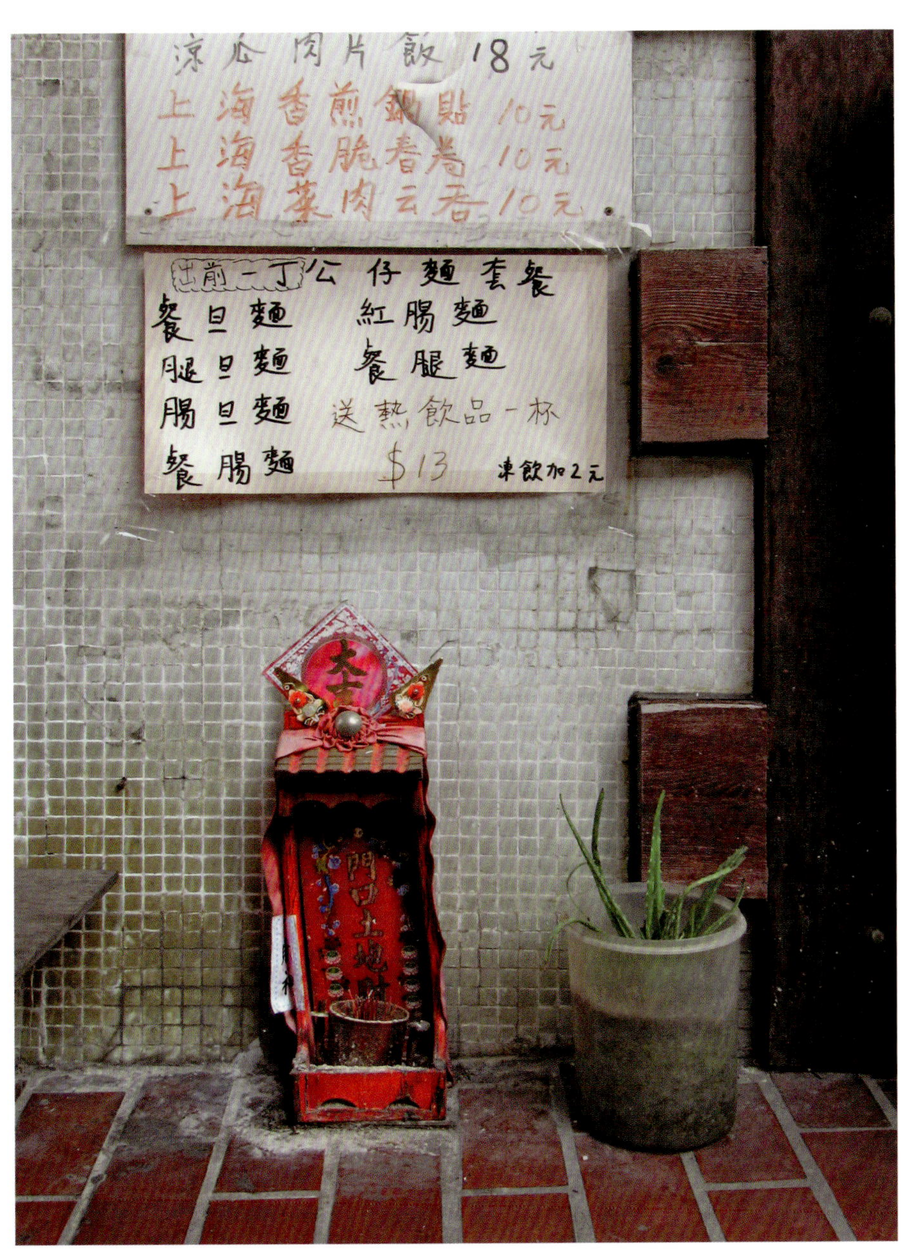
涼心肉片飯 18元
上海香煎鍋貼 10元
上海香脆春卷 10元
上海菜肉云吞 10元
出前一丁 公仔麵套餐
餐旦麵　　紅腸麵
腿旦麵　　餐腿麵
腸旦麵　送熱飲品一杯
餐腸麵　　$13　凍飲加2元
本
門口土地財神

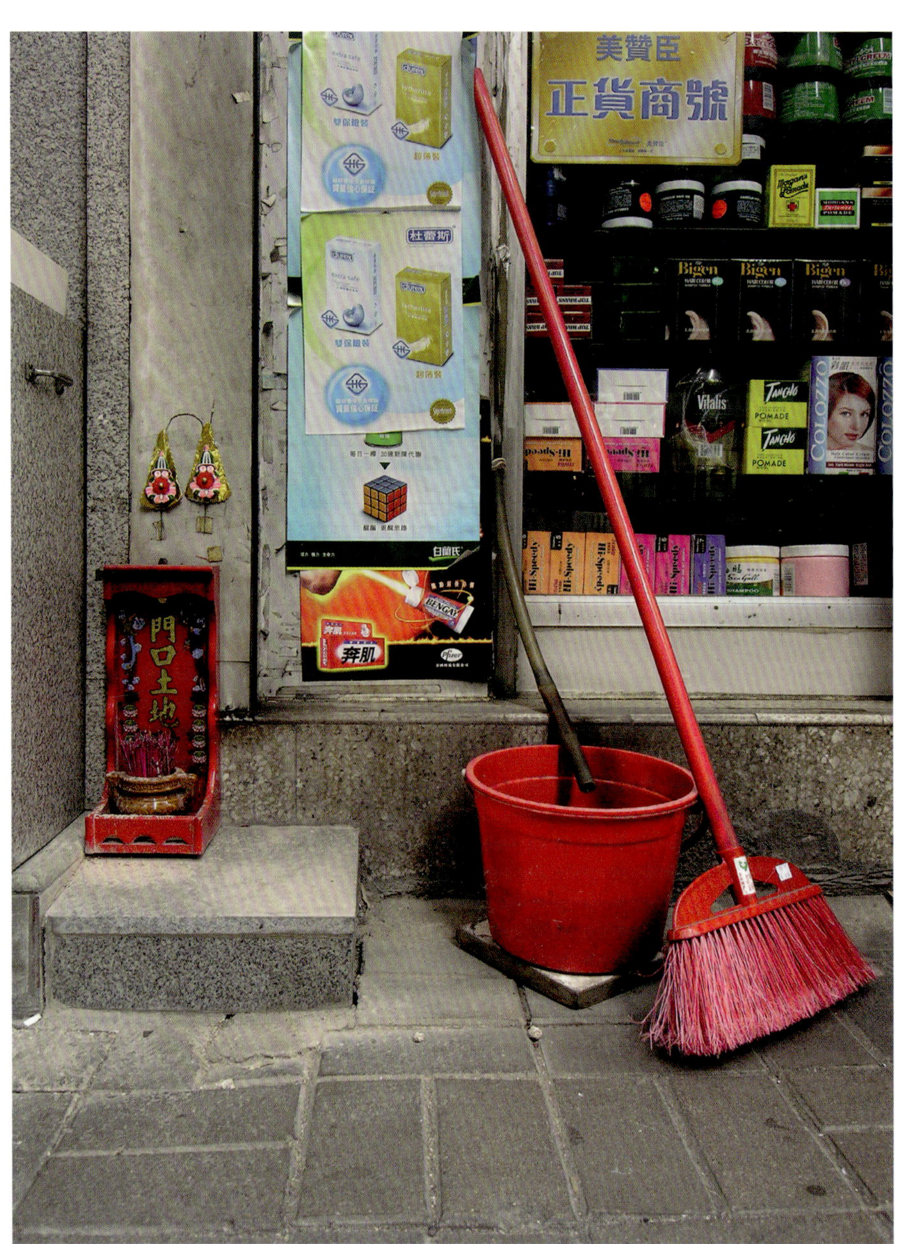

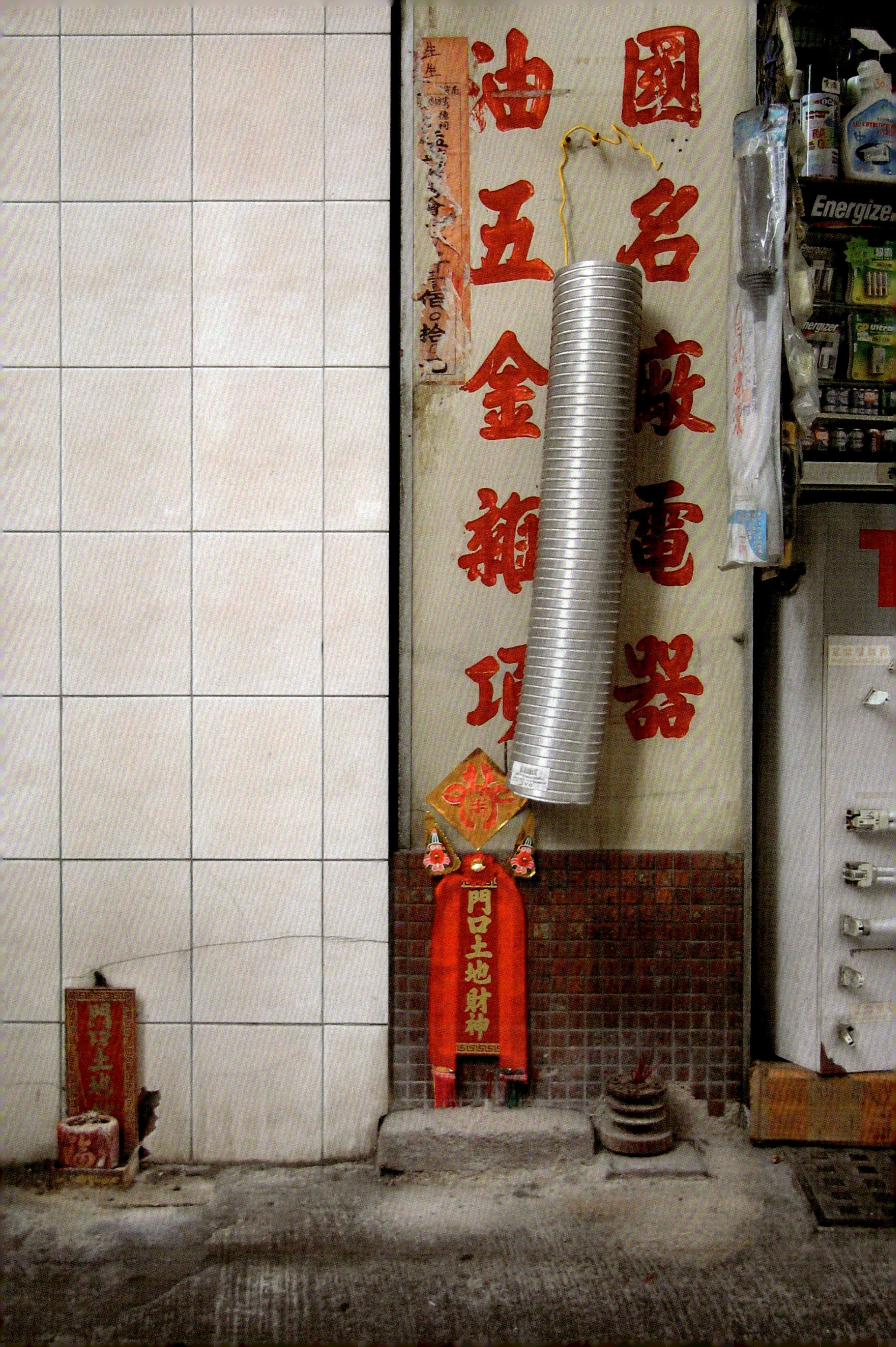
國名廠電器
油五金雜項
門口土地財神
門口土地財神
Energizer

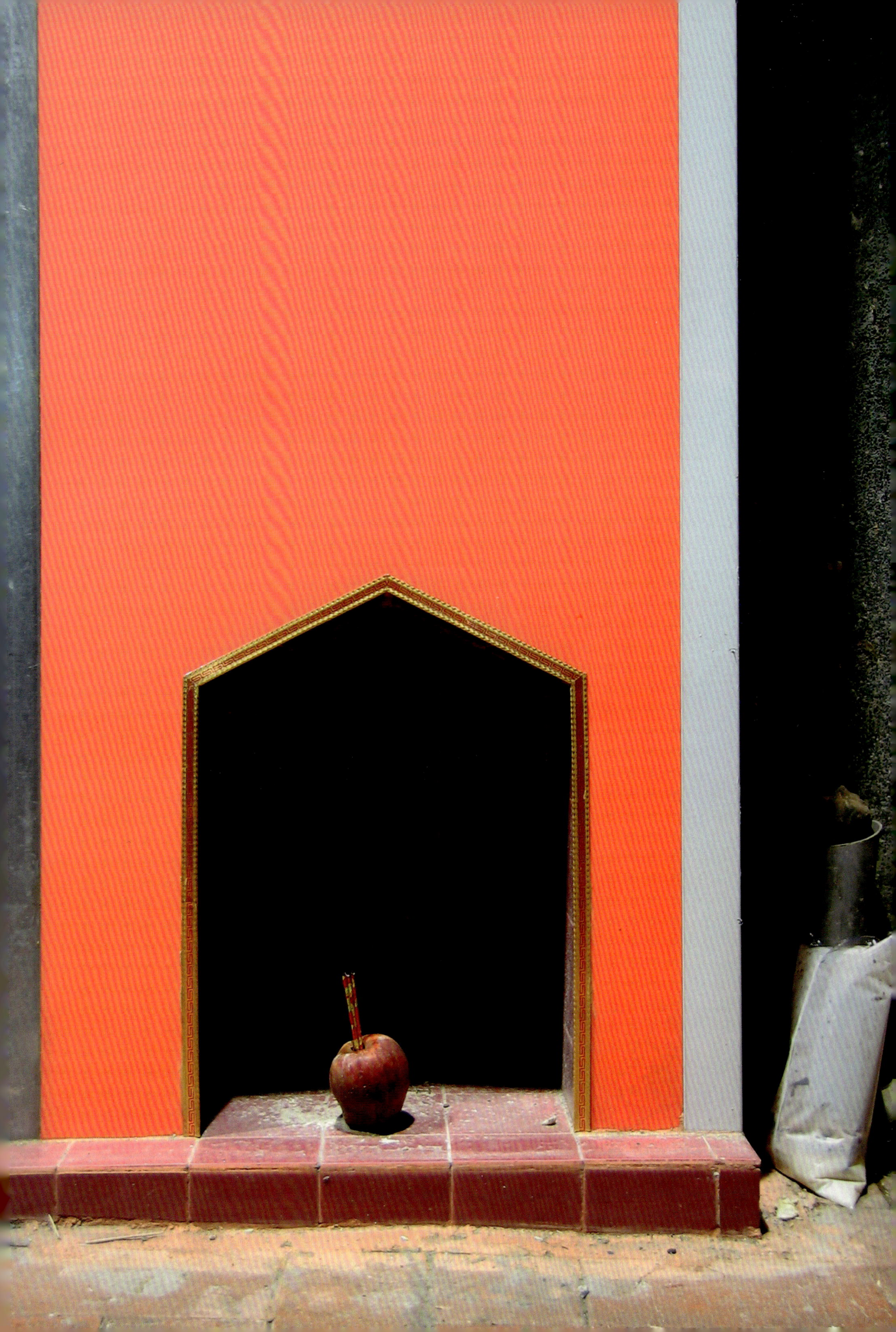

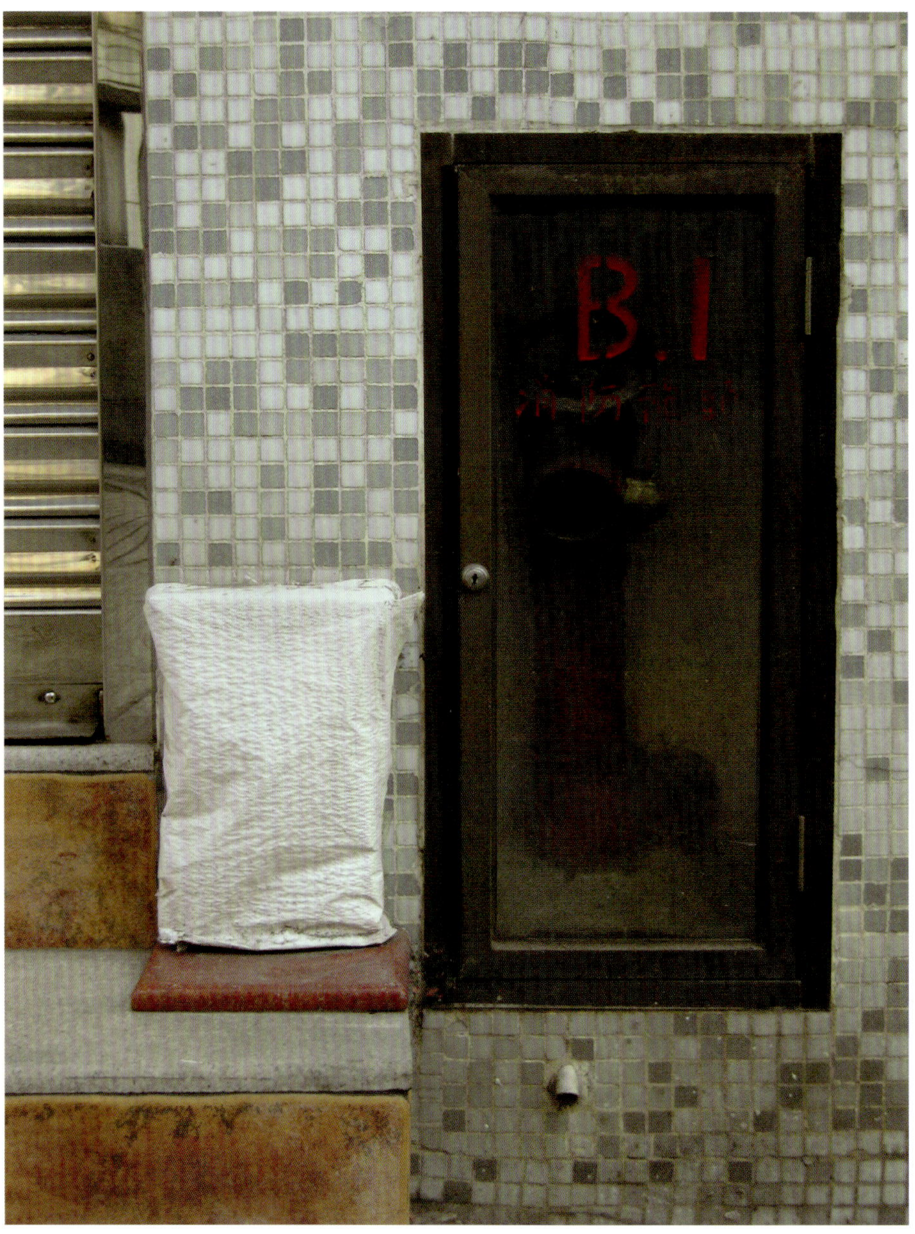

B.1

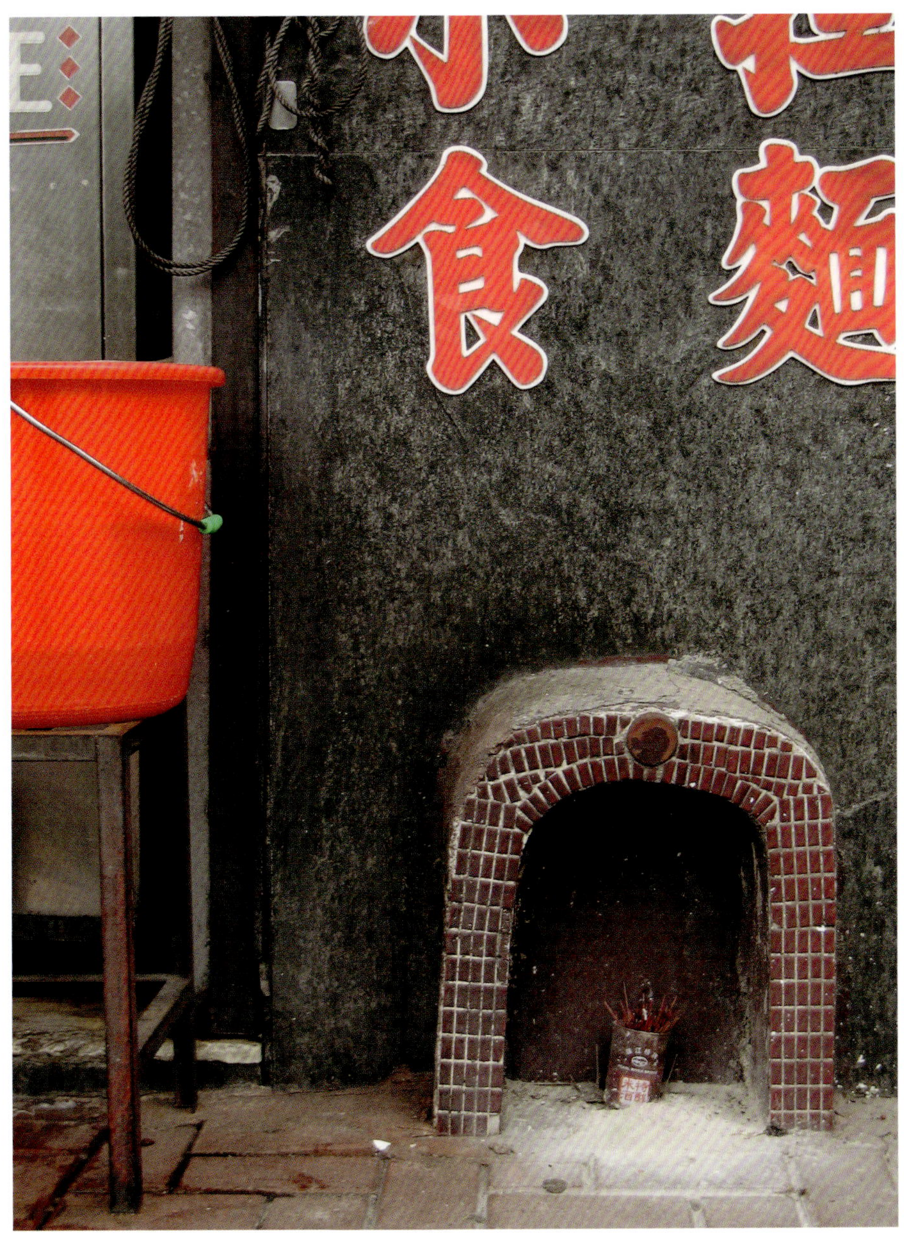

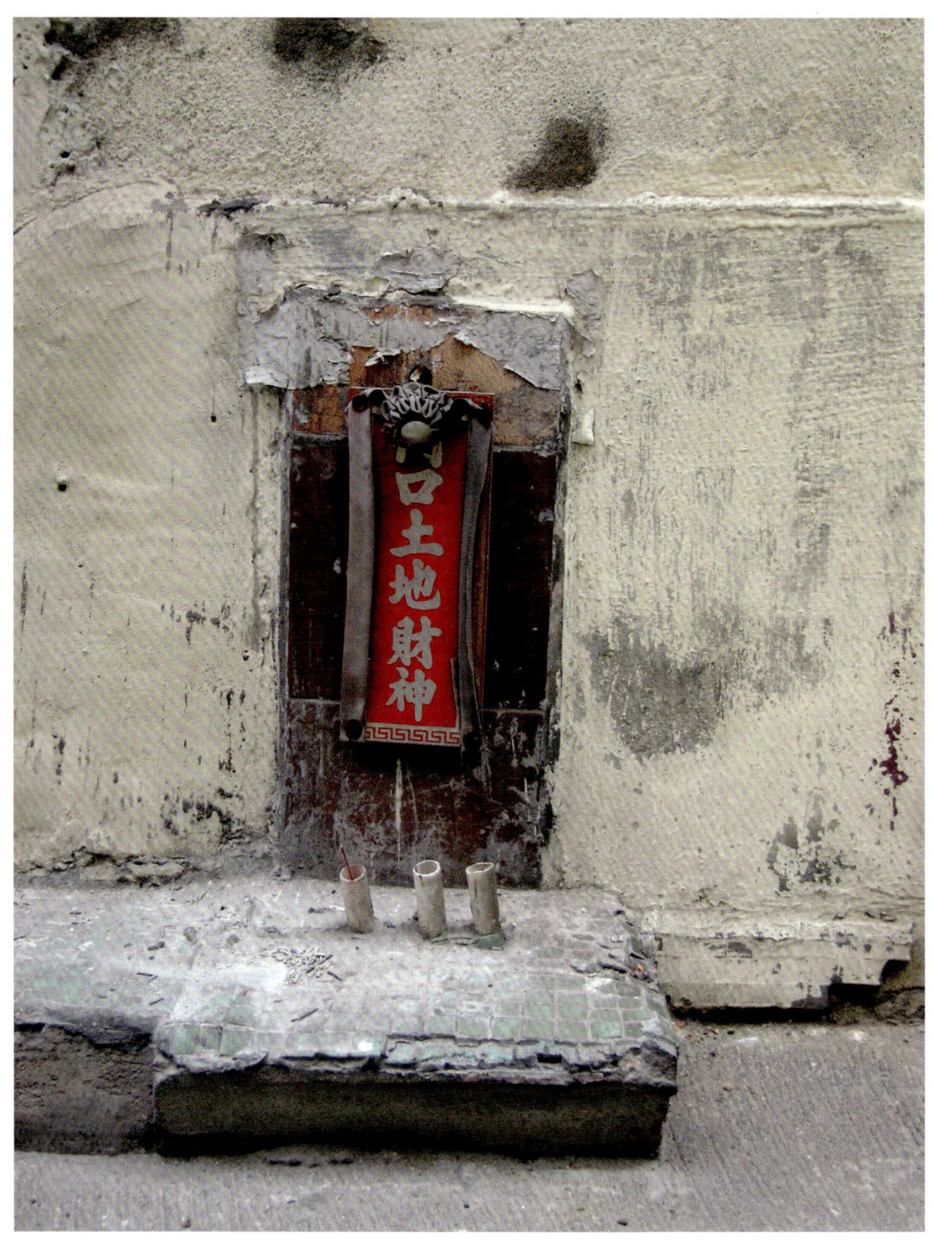

口土地財神

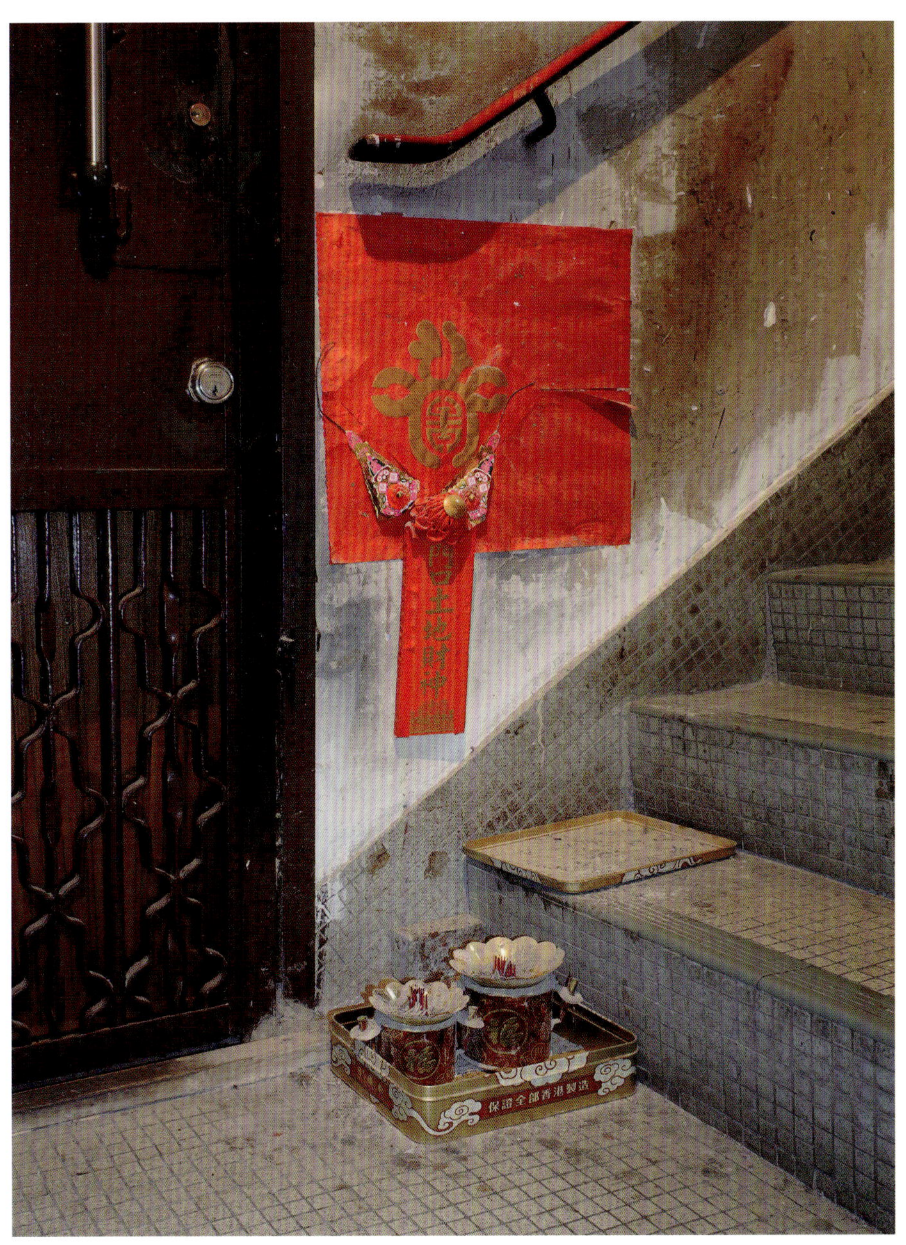

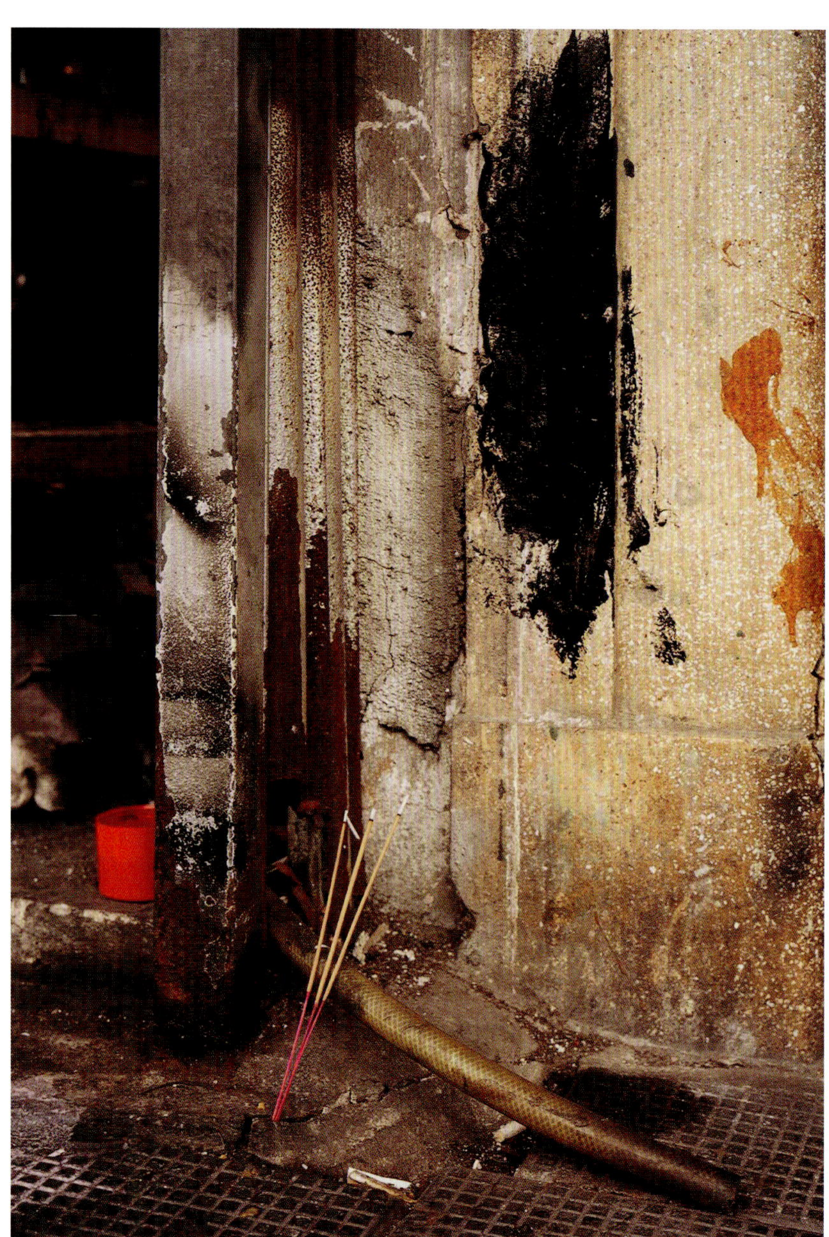

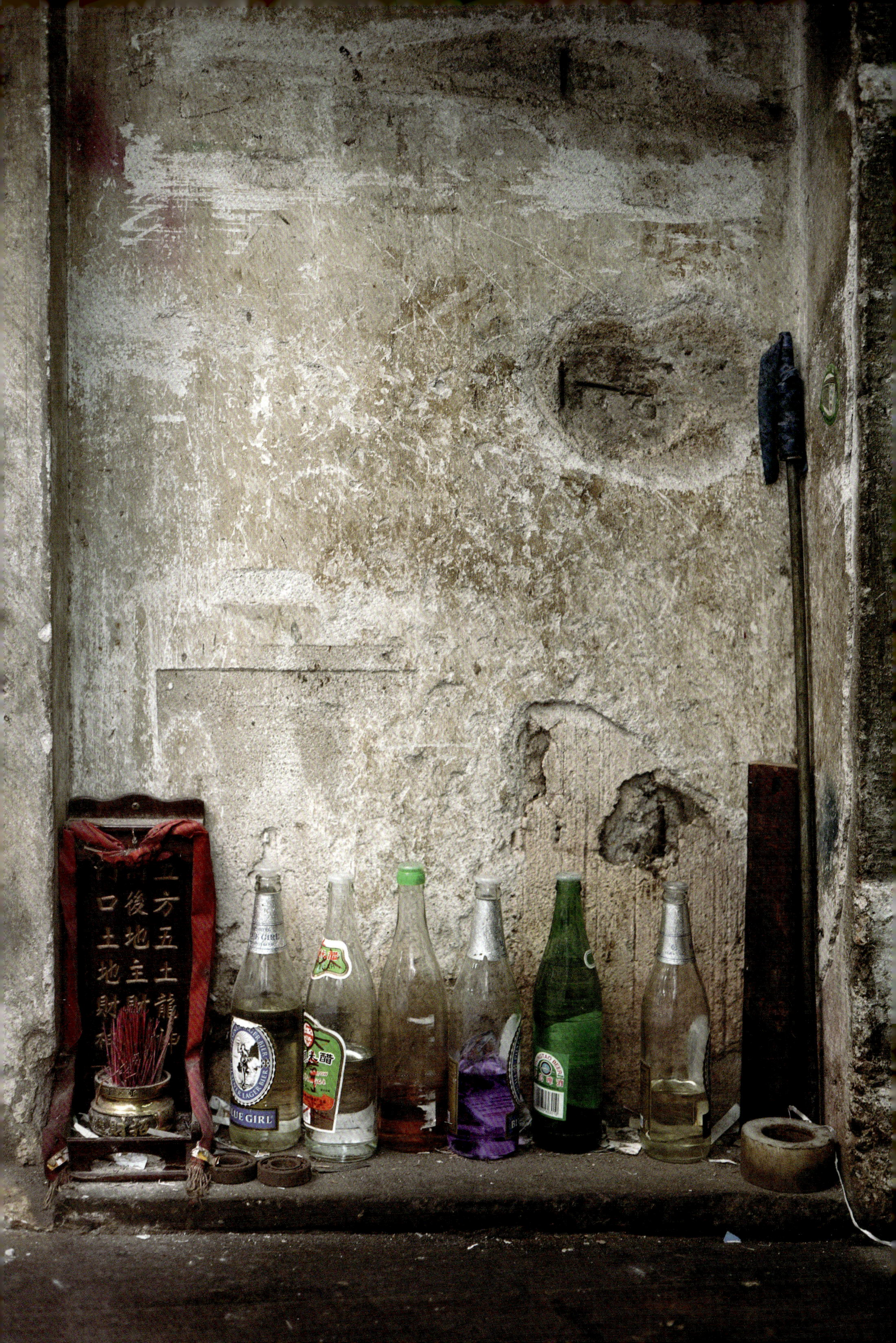
五方五土龍神
前後地主財神
口土地財神
BLUE GIRL

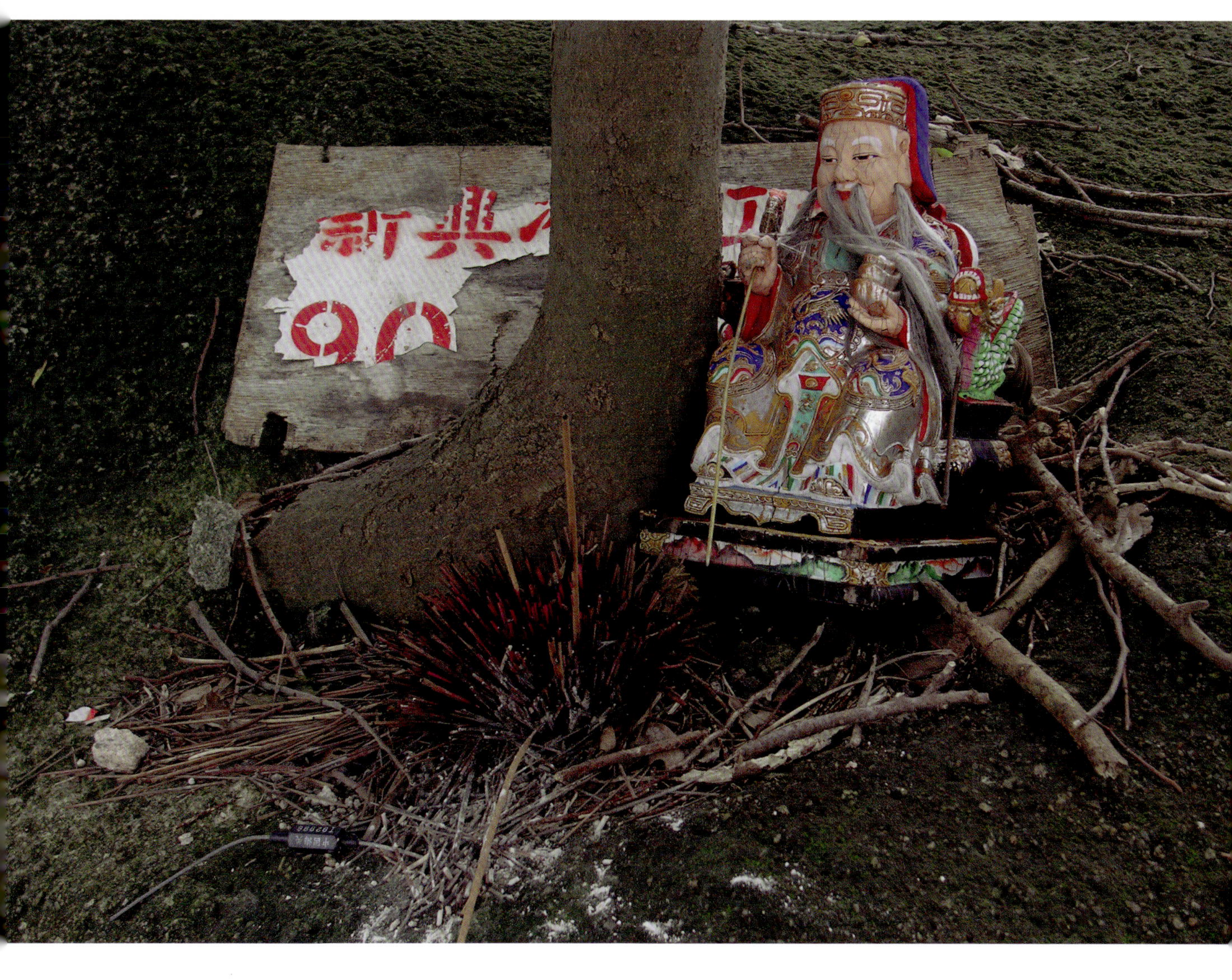

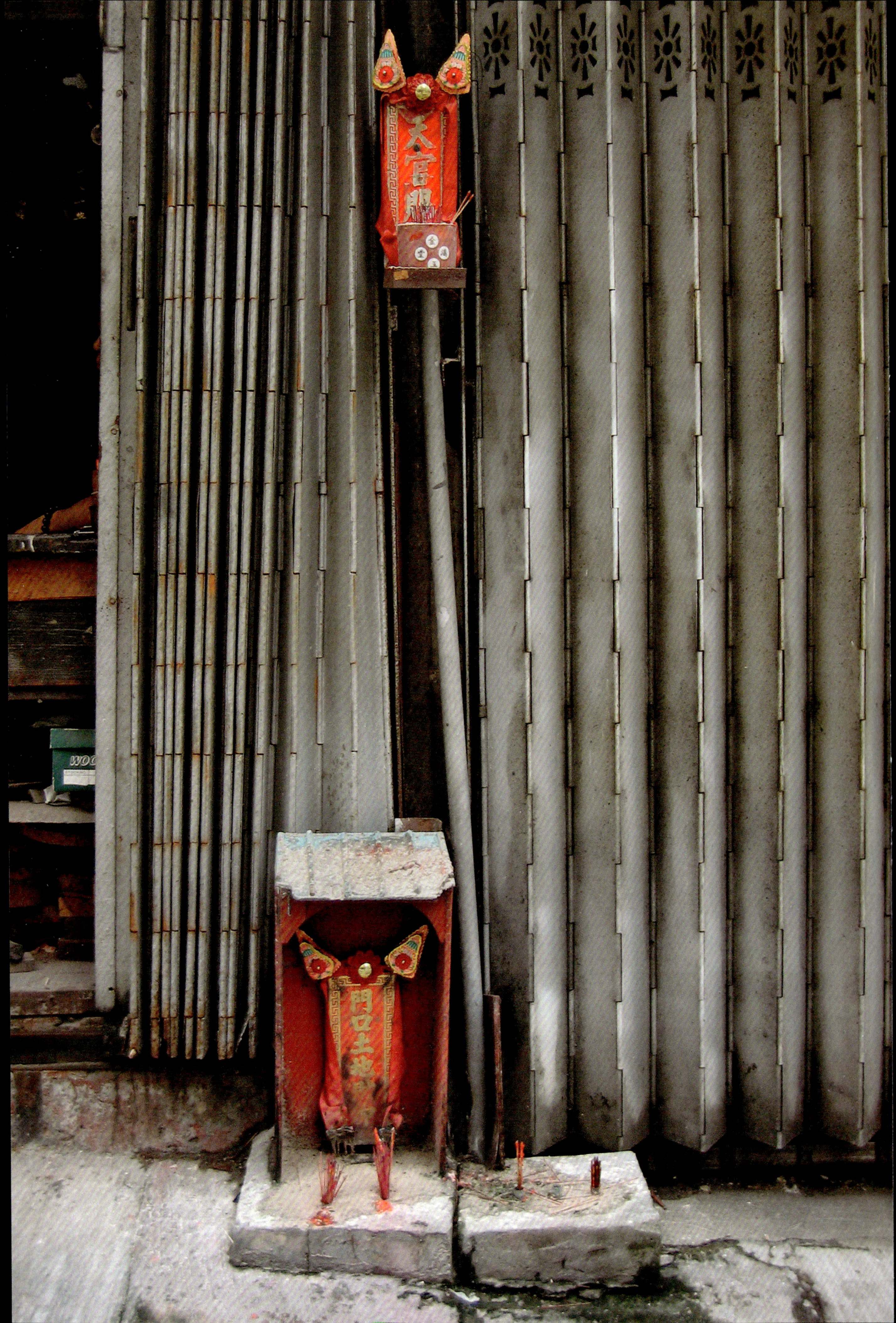

天官賜福
門口土地財神

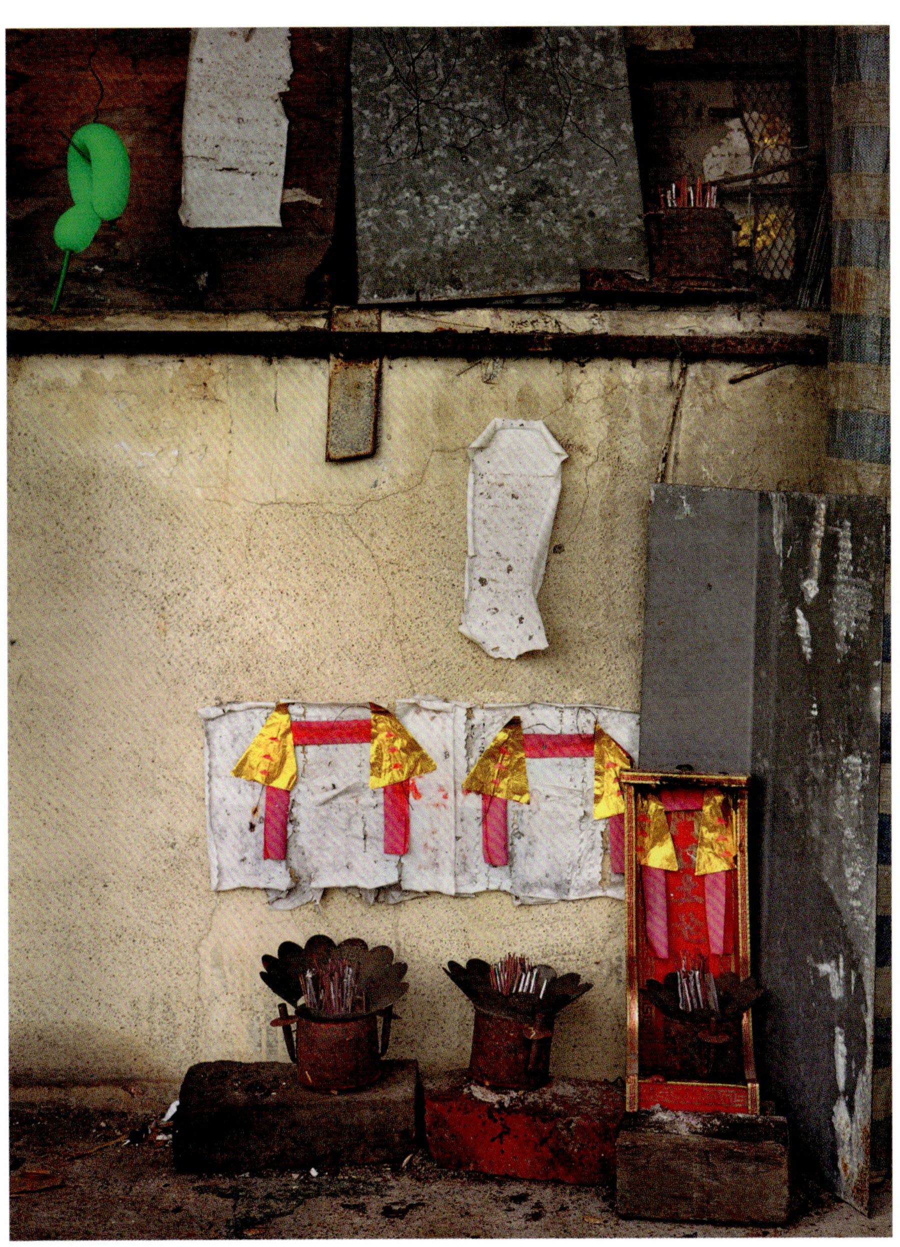

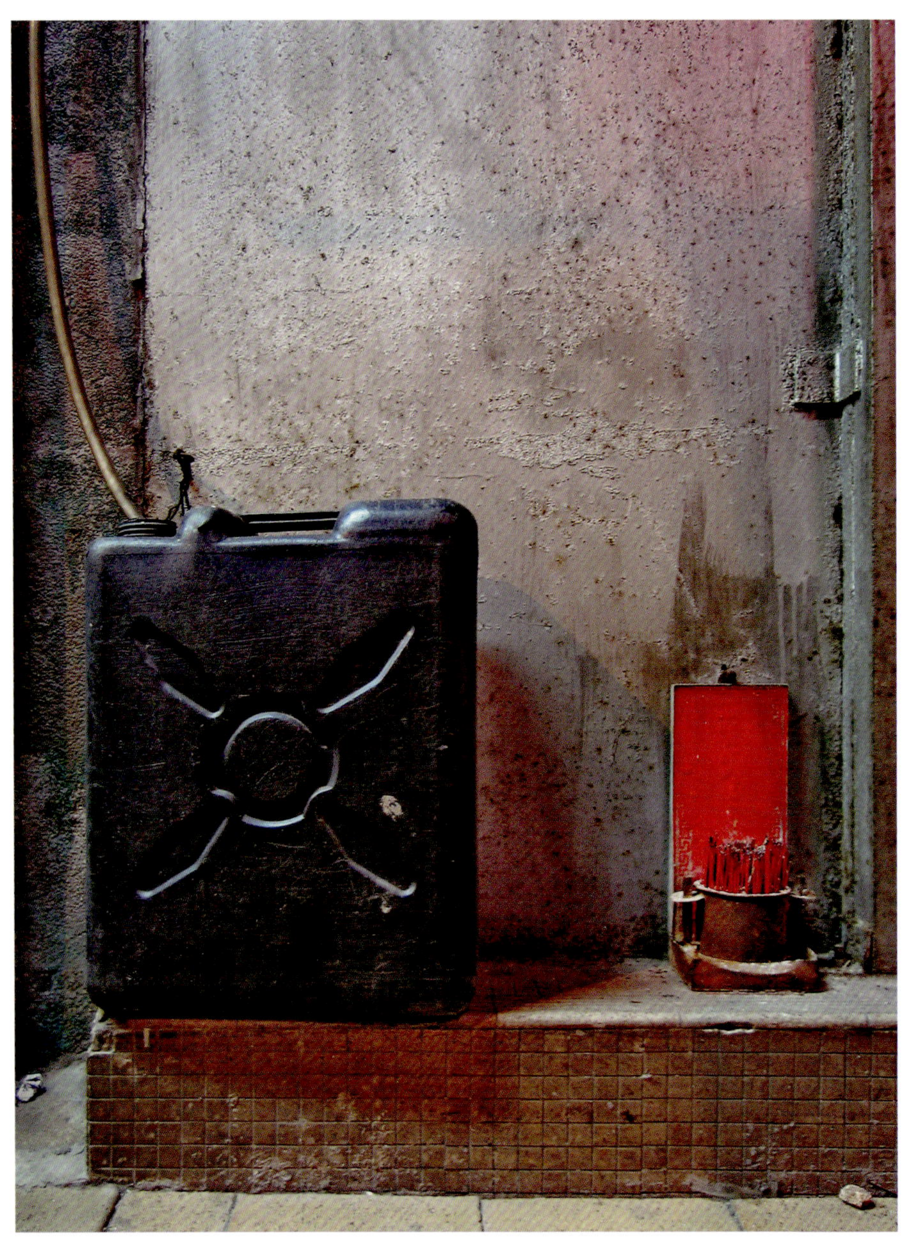

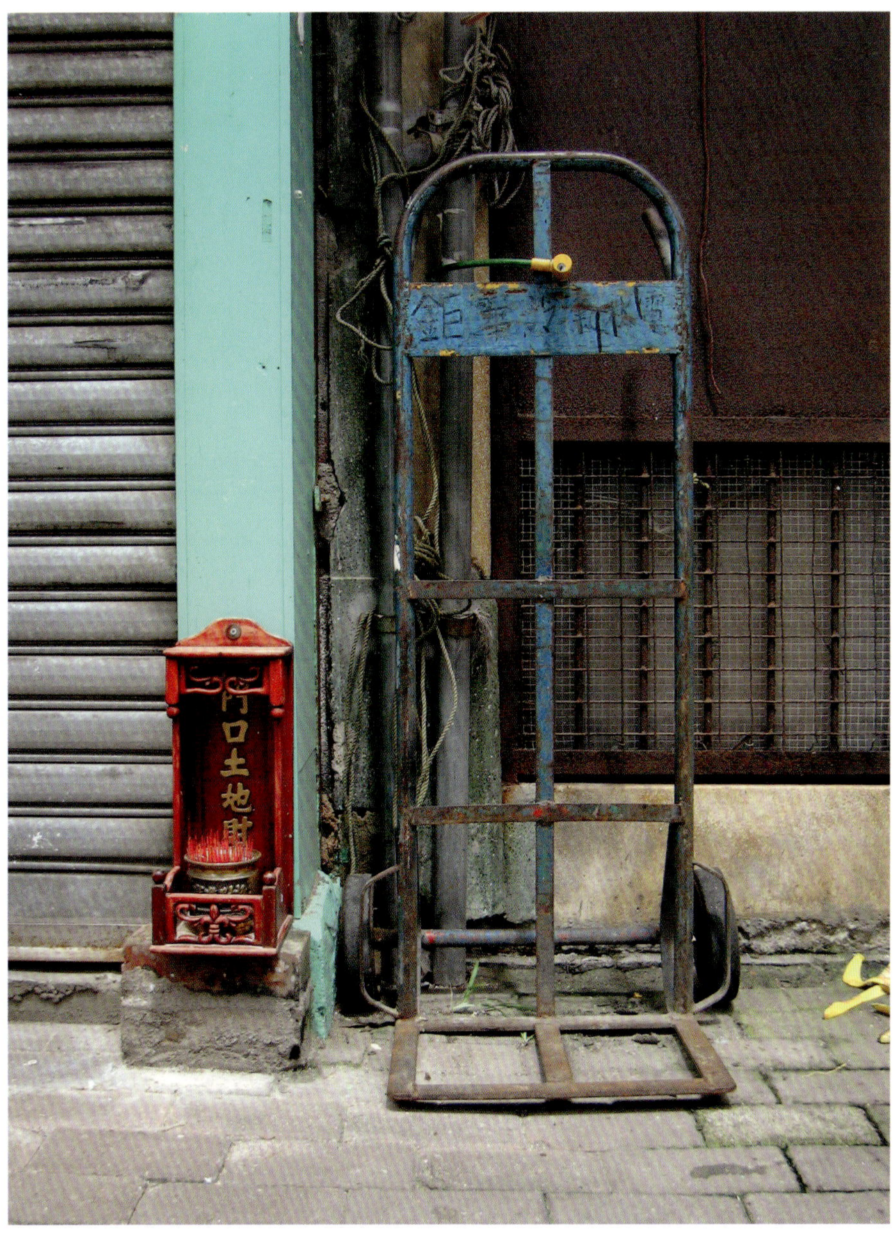

門口土地財

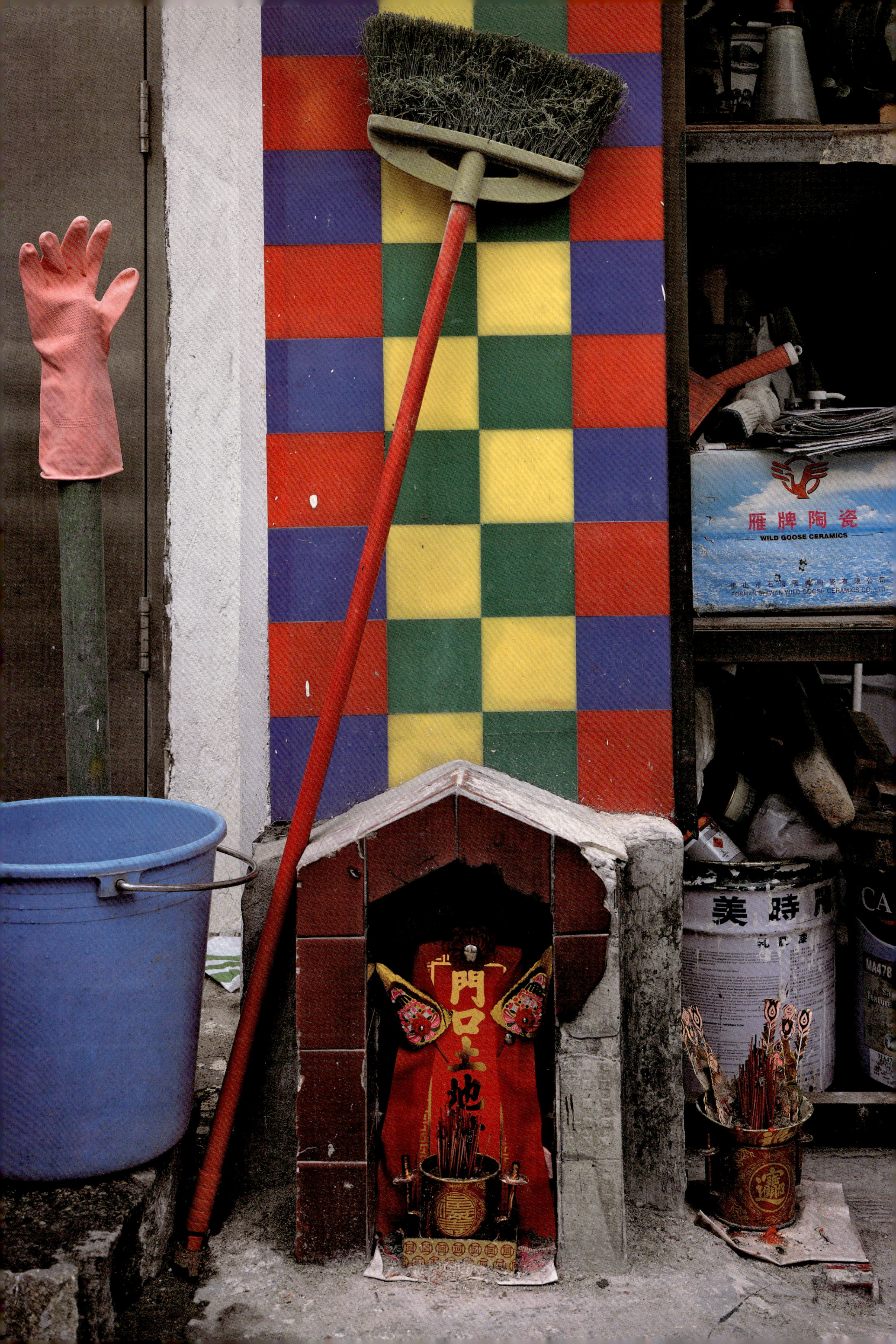

雁牌陶瓷
WILD GOOSE CERAMICS
佛山市石湾雁牌陶瓷有限公司
FOSHAN SHIWAN WILD GOOSE CERAMICS CO.,LTD.
美時門
門口土地

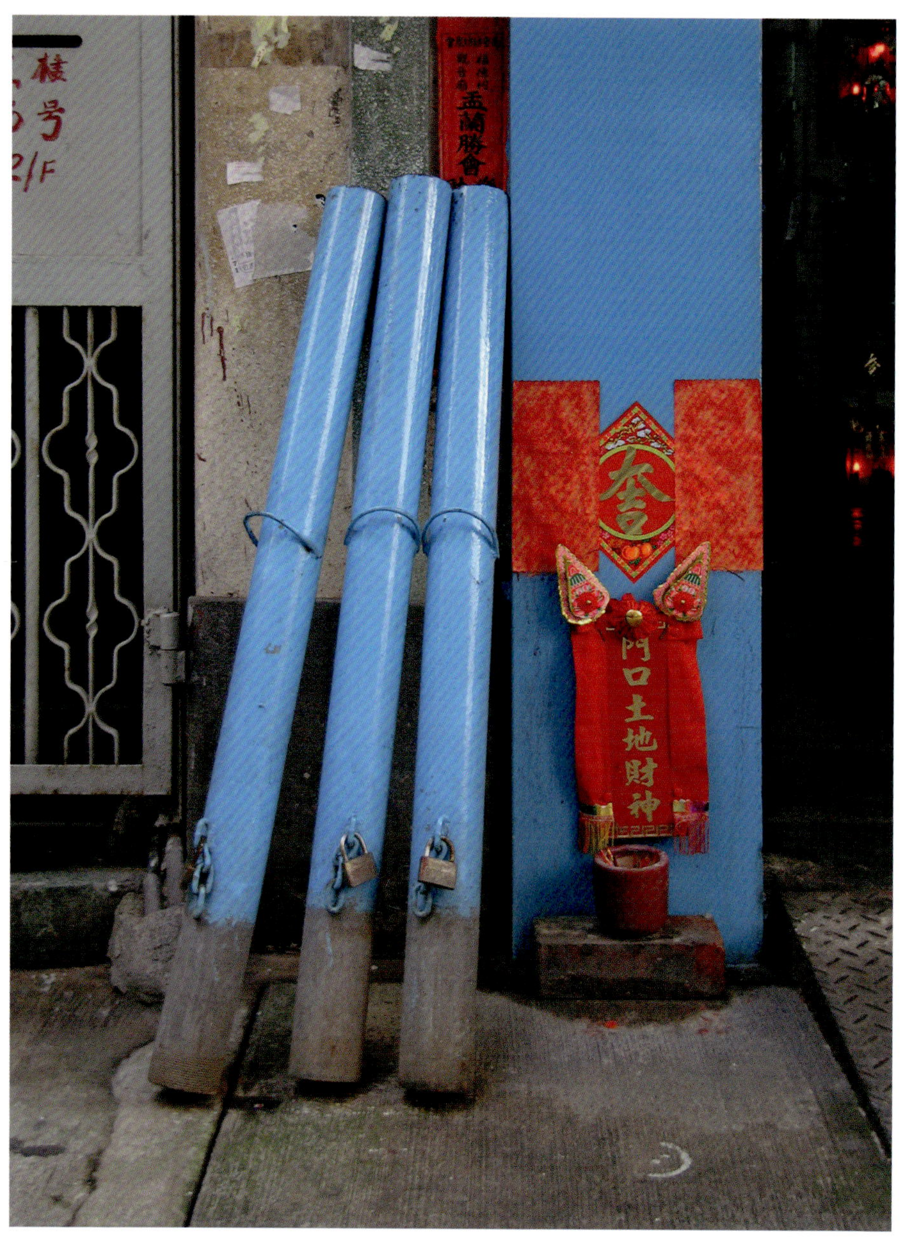

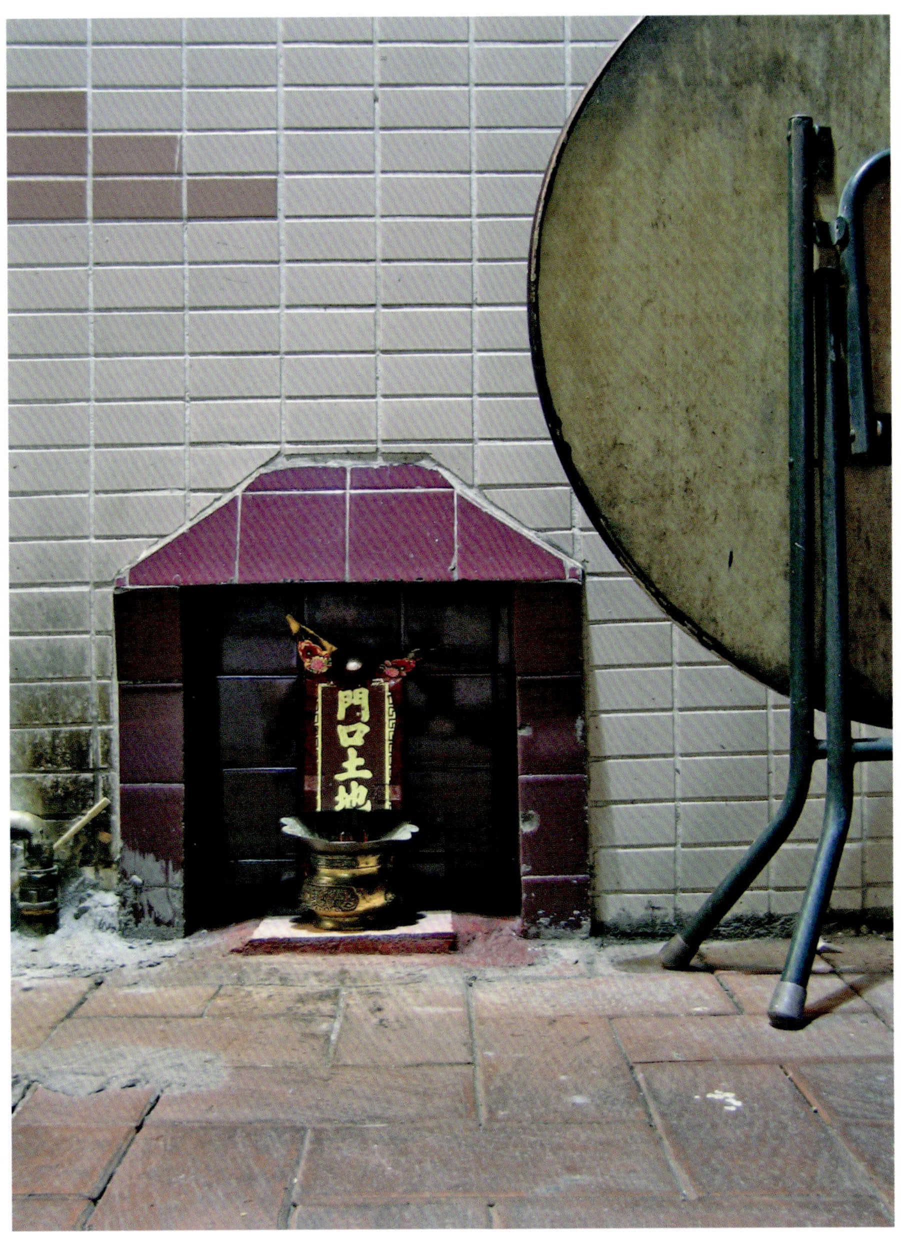

門口土地

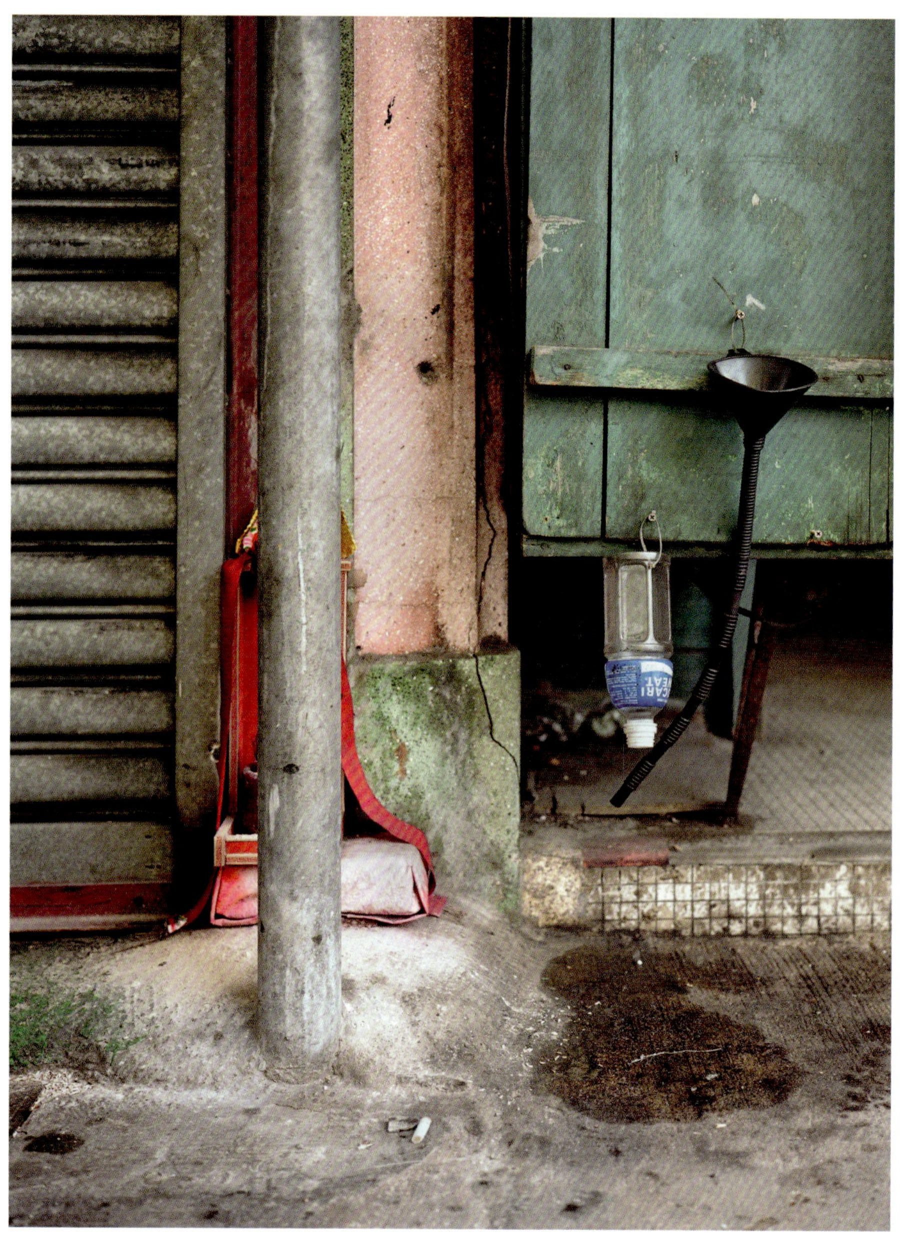

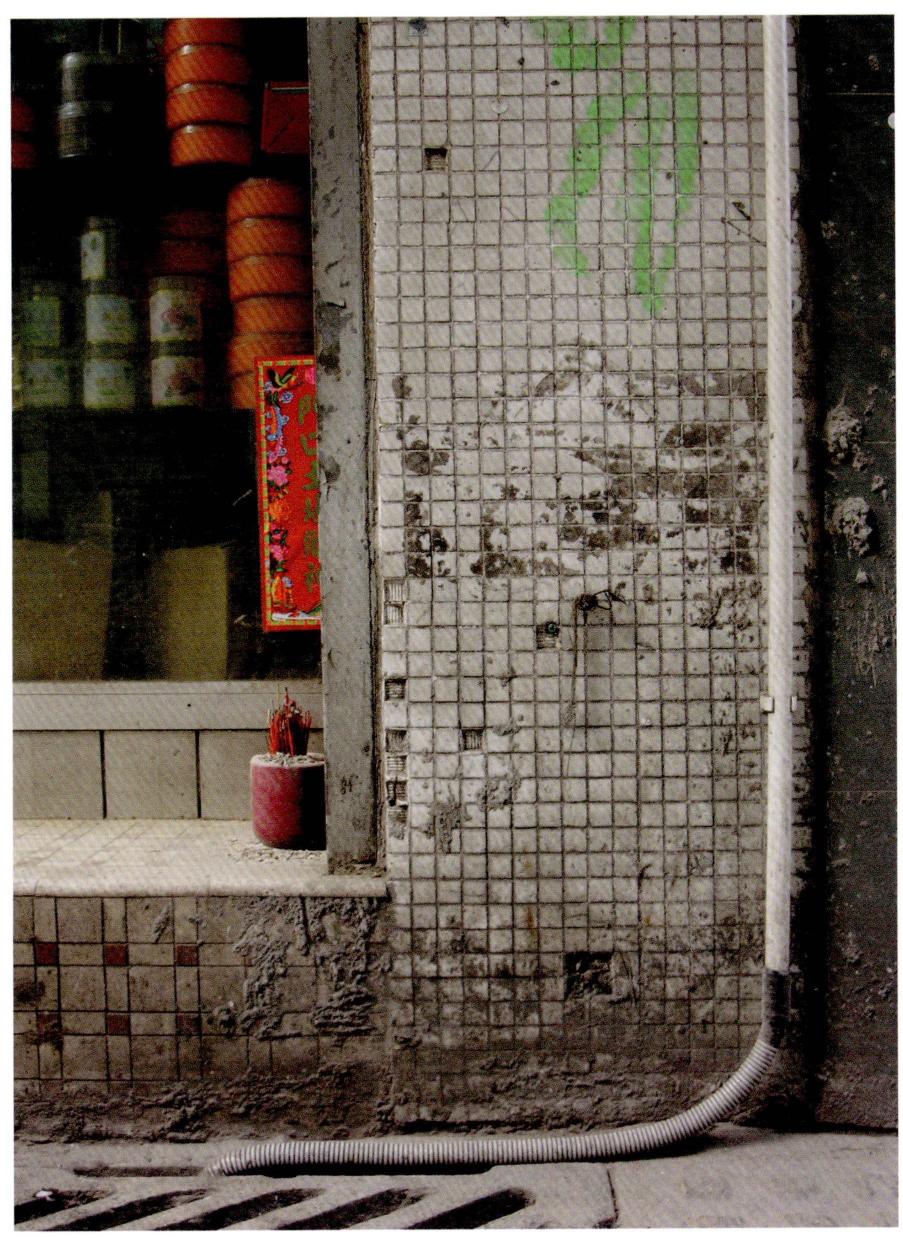

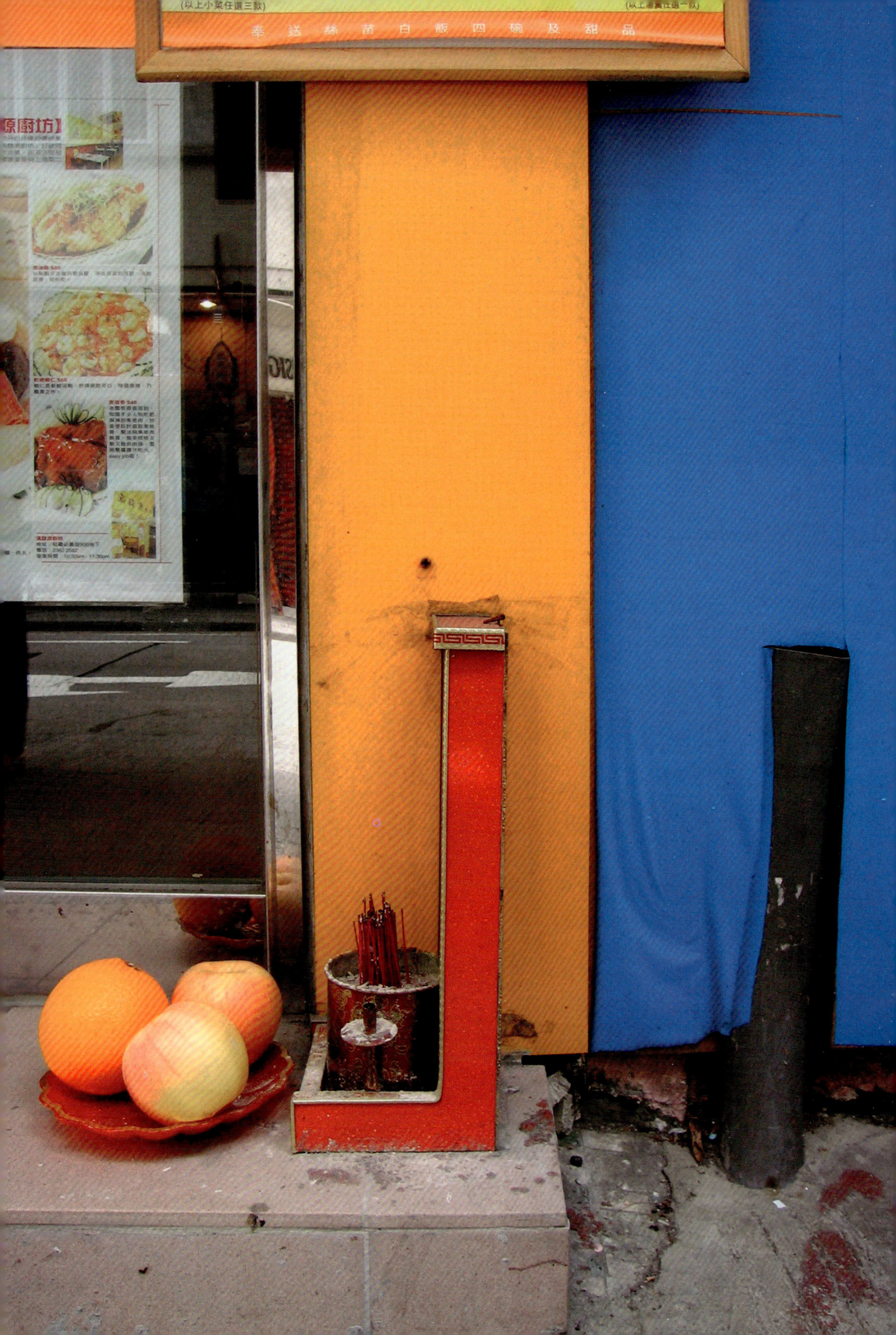

奉　送　絲　苗　白　飯　四　碗　及　甜　品
(以上小菜任選三款)
(以上湯羹任送一款)
原廚坊

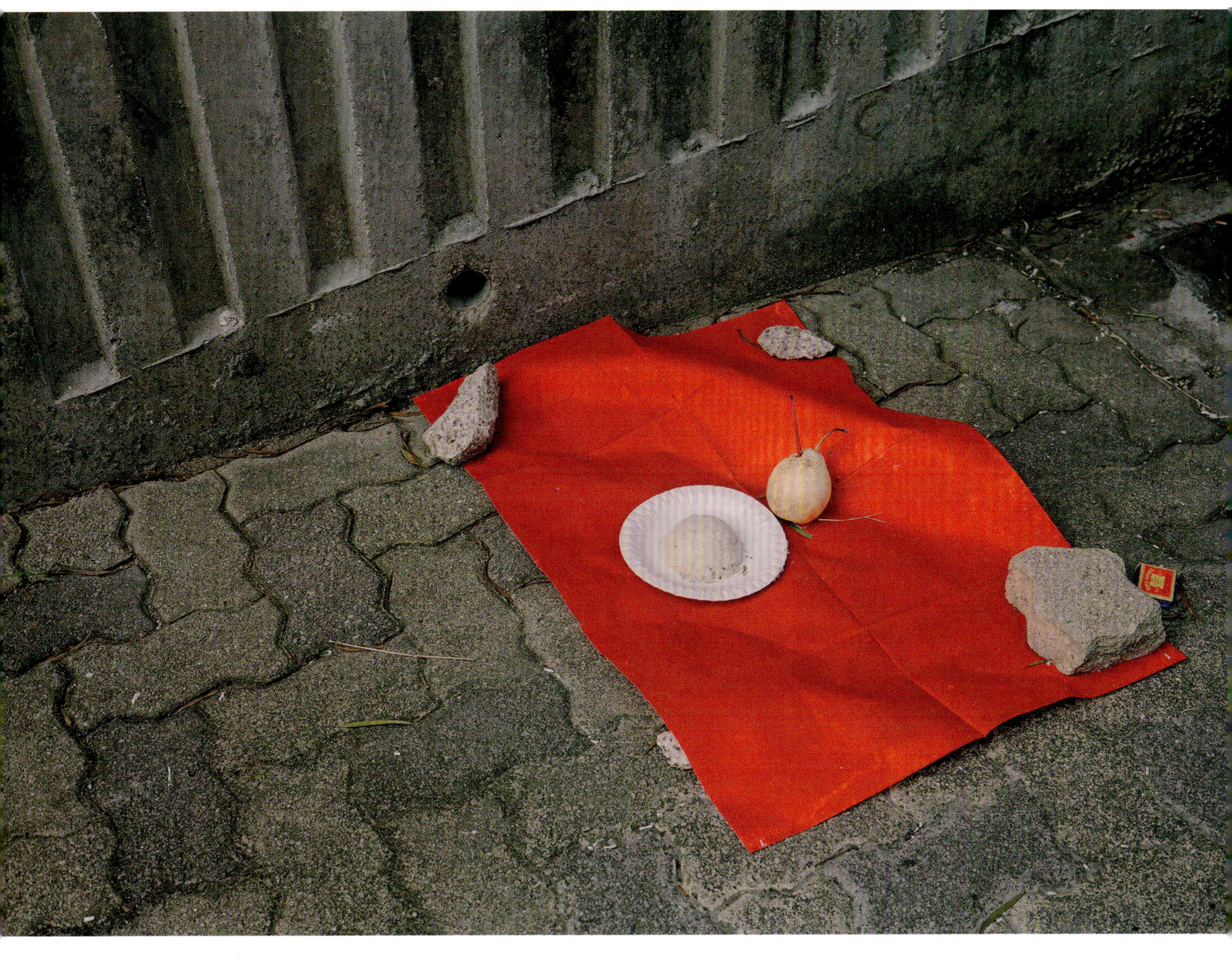

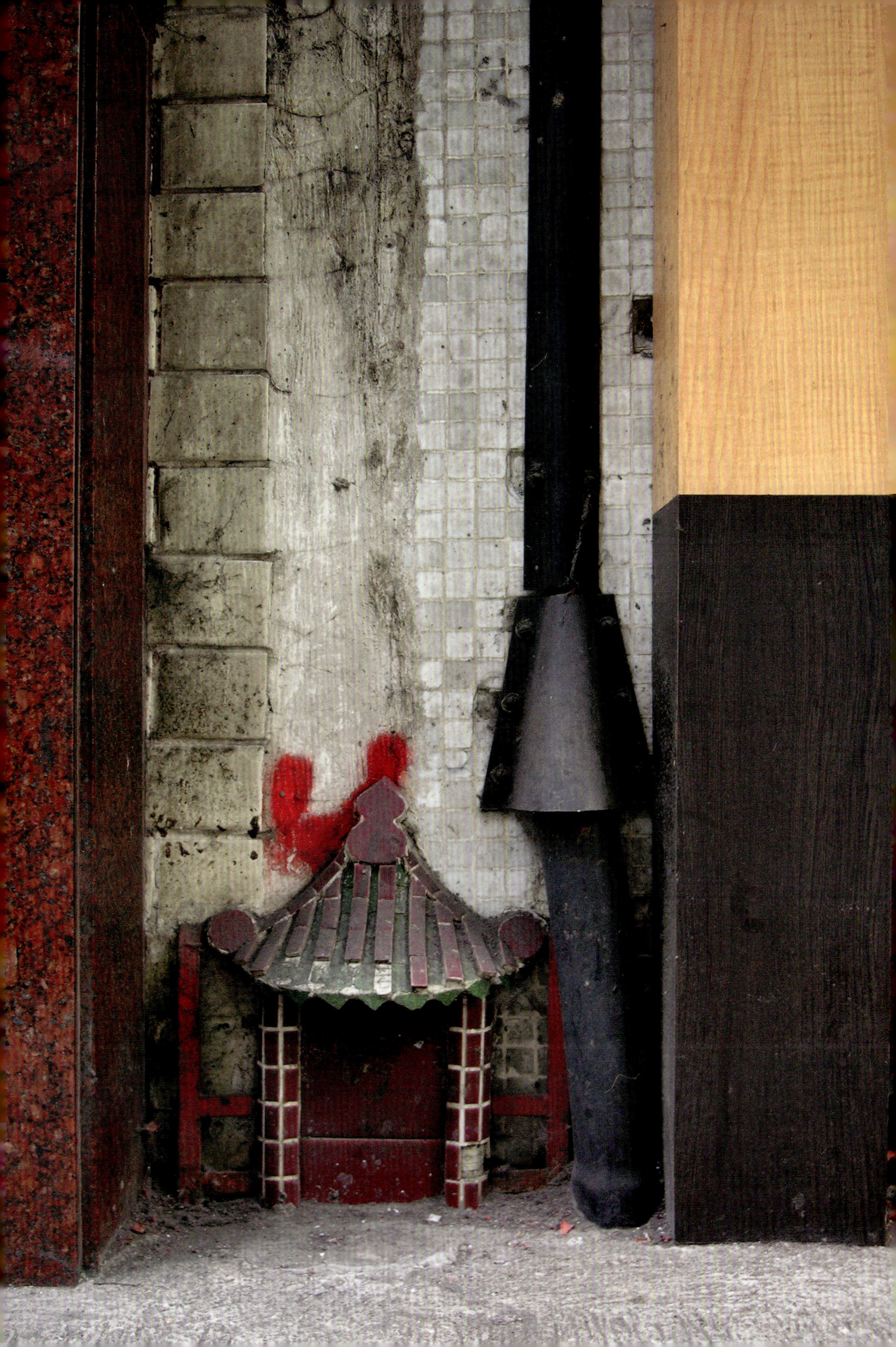

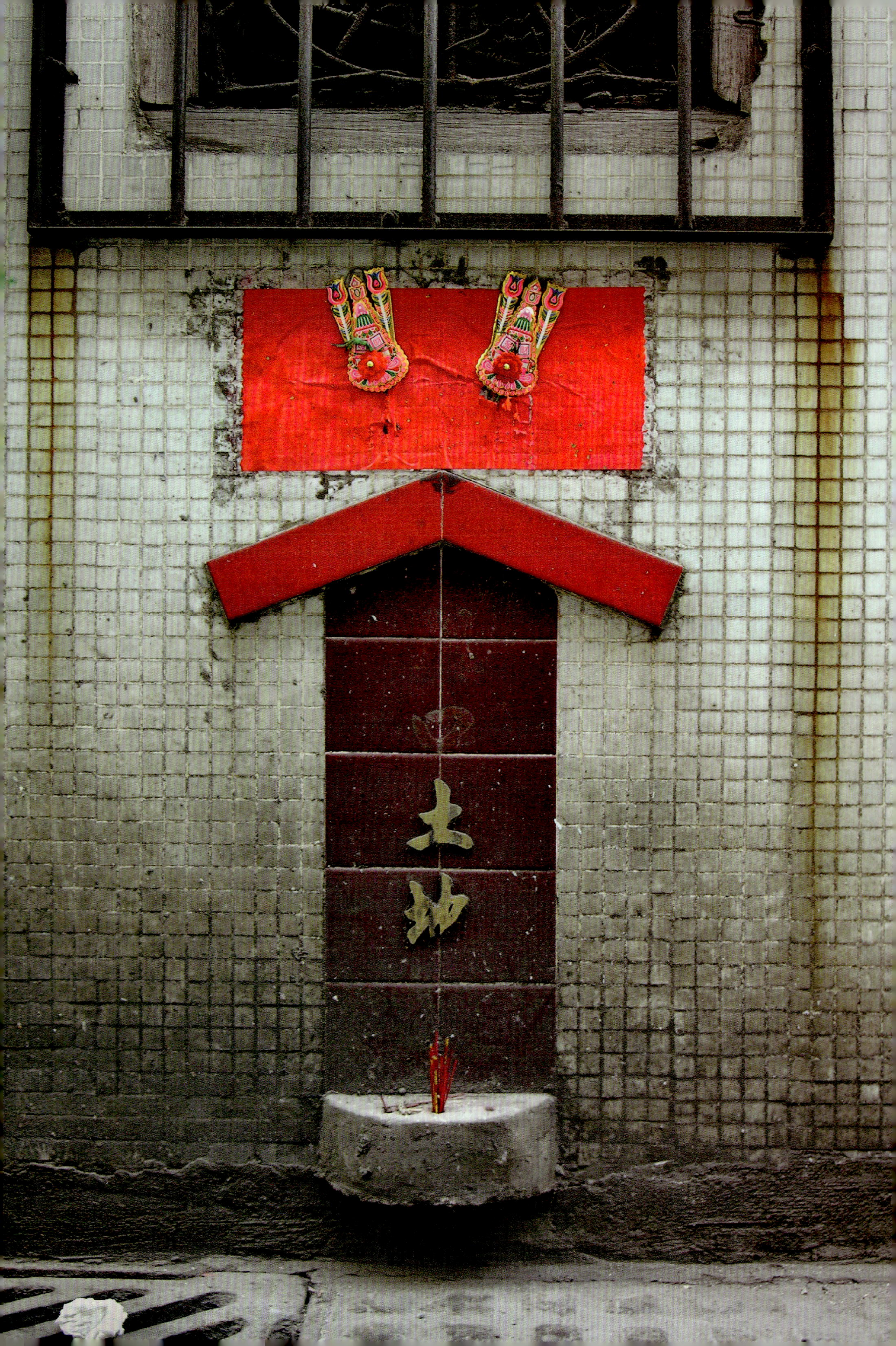

土地

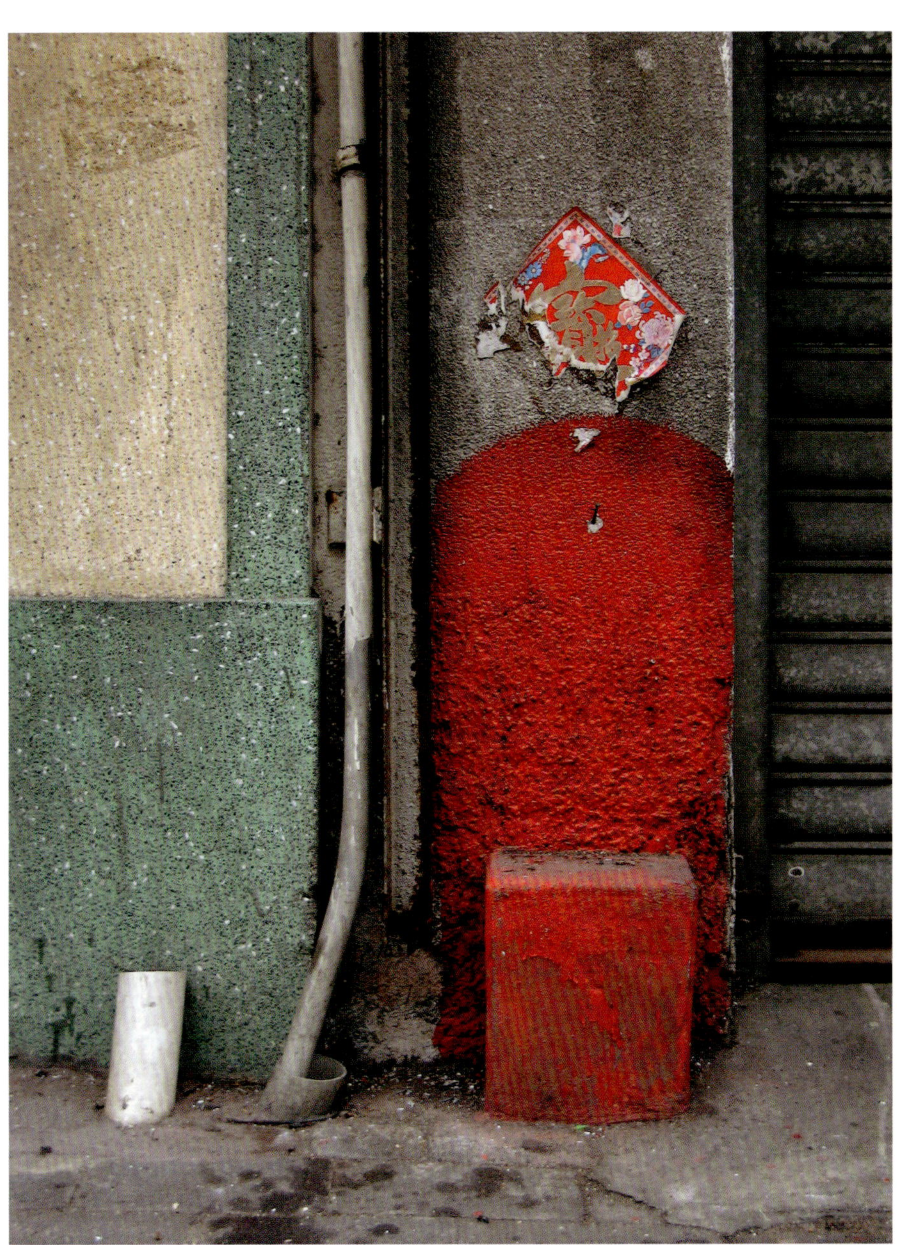

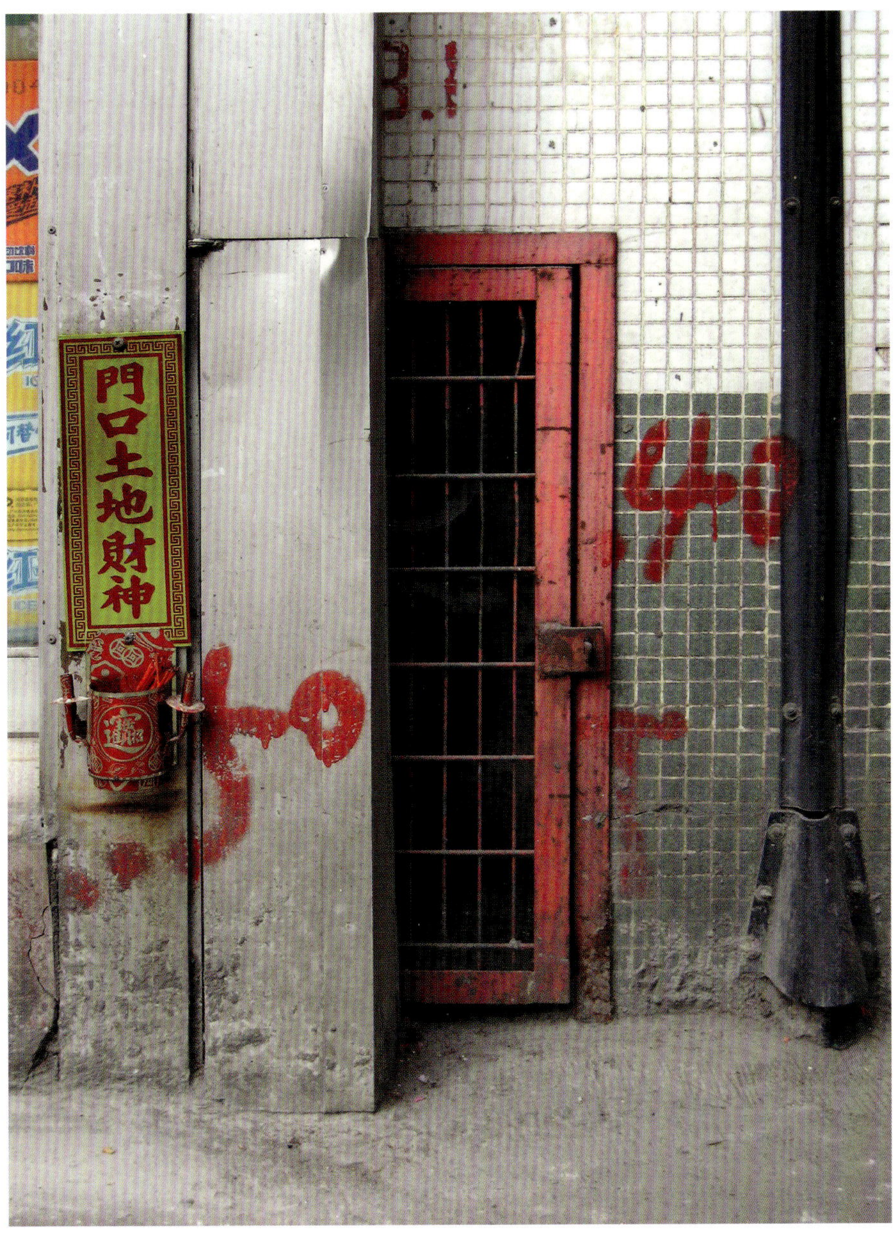
門口土地財神

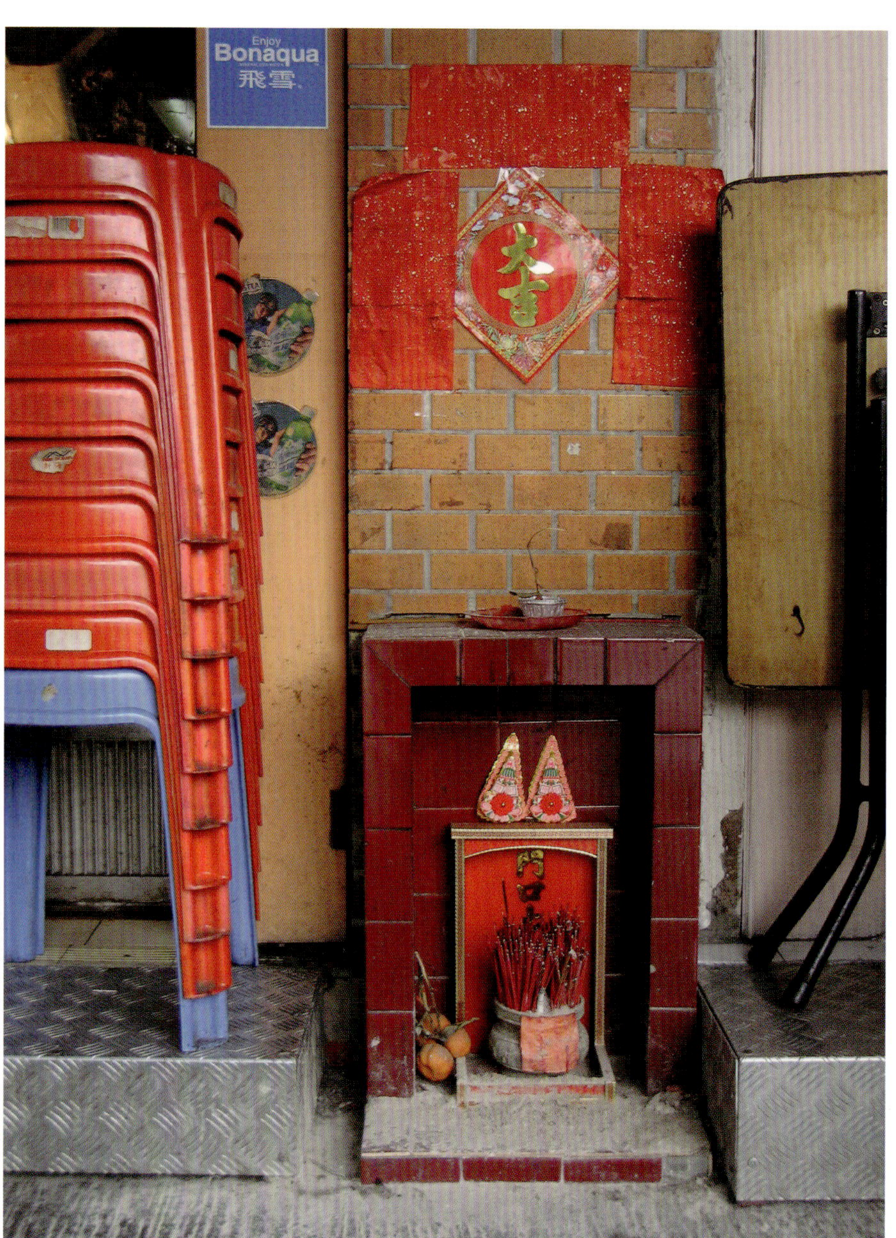

Enjoy
Bonaqua
飛雪
大吉
門口土地財神

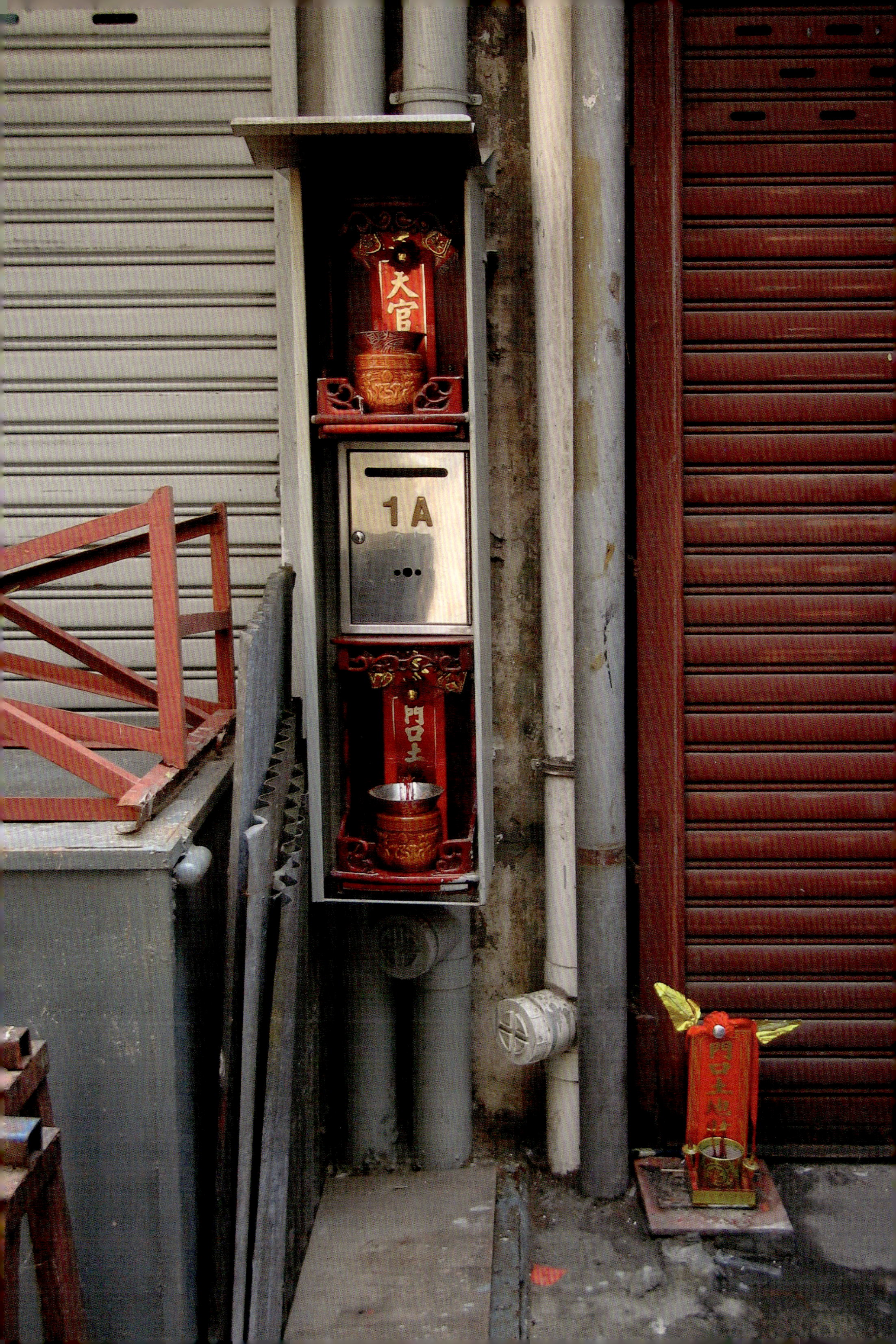

天官
1A
門口土
門口土地財神

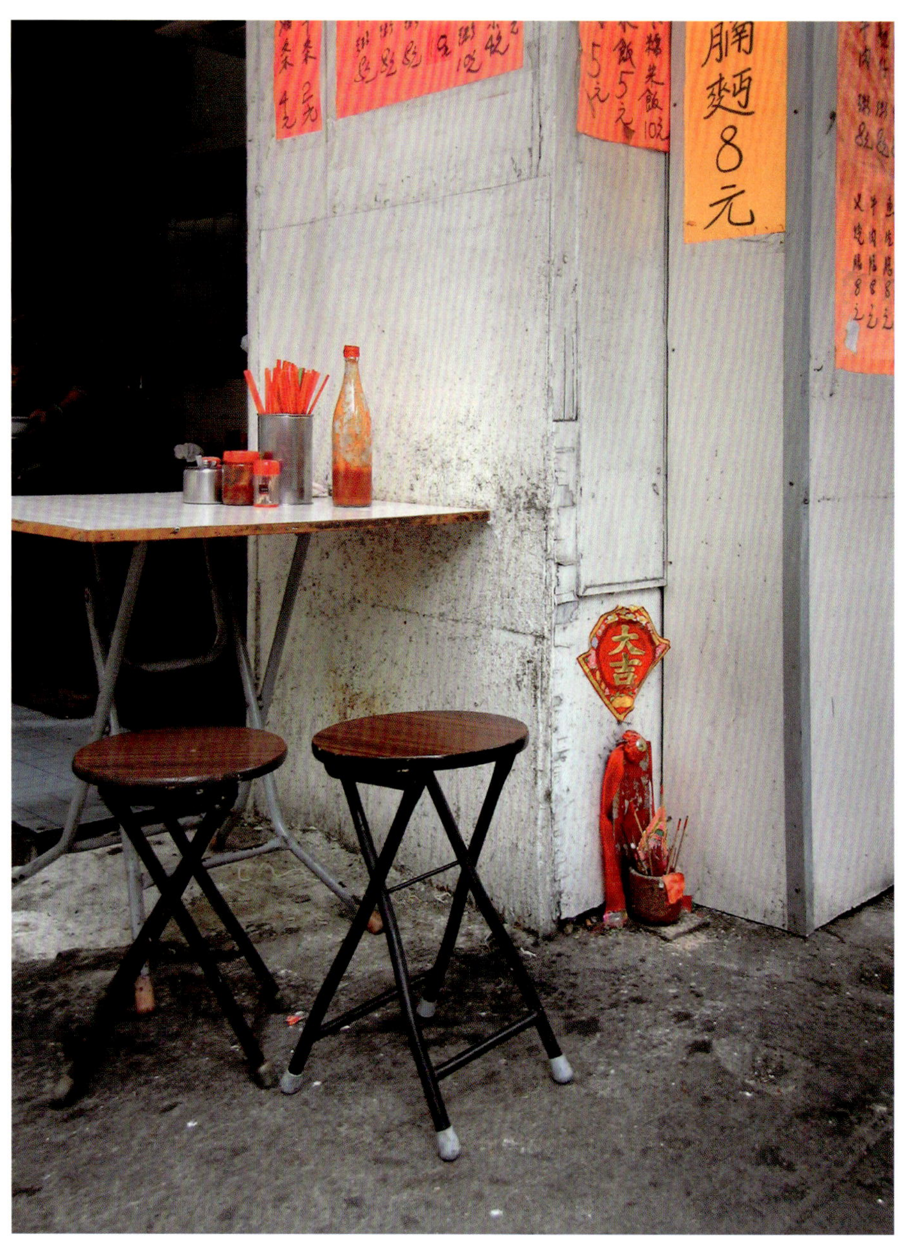
開
麵
8
元
大吉

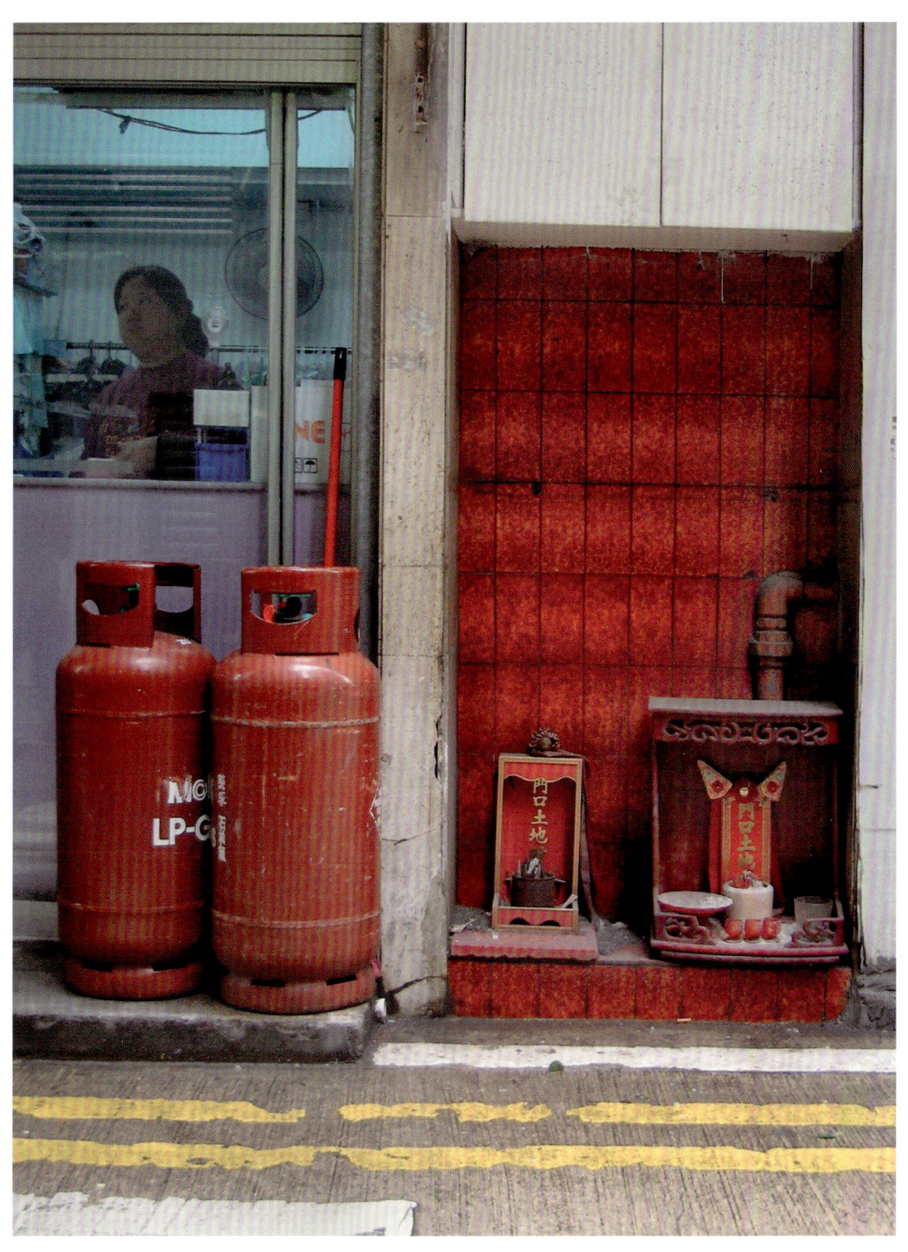
LP-G
門口土地
門口土地

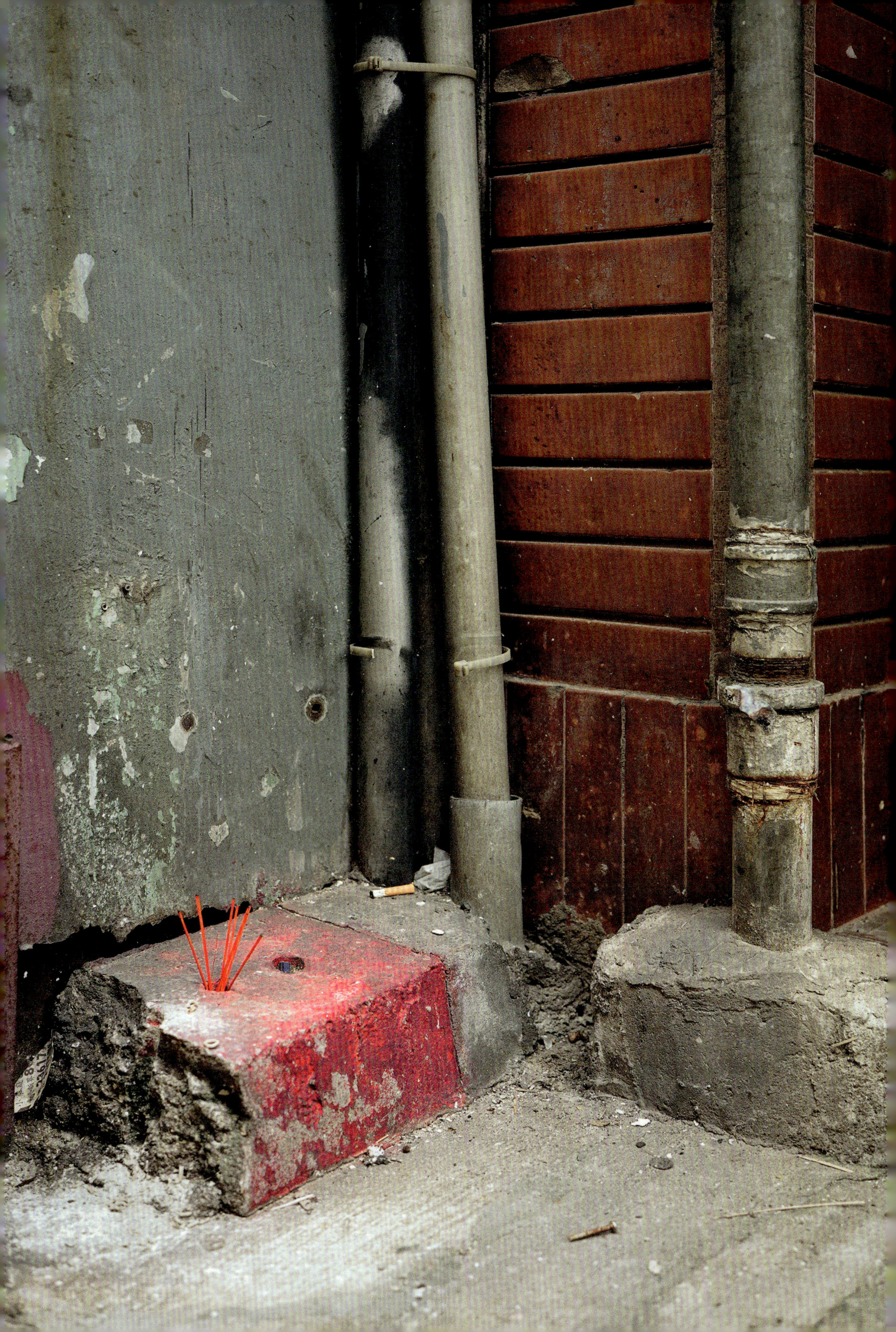

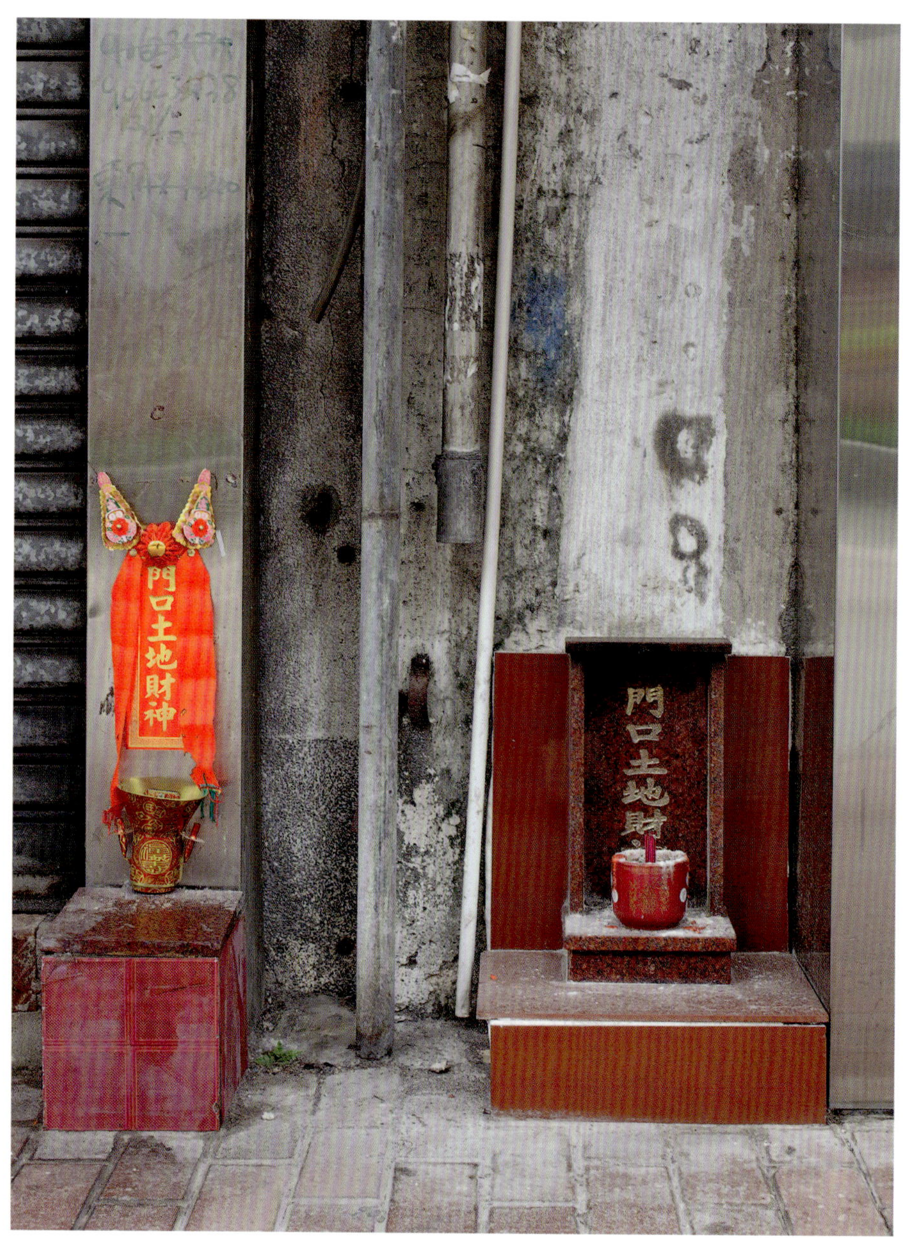

門口土地財神
門口土地財

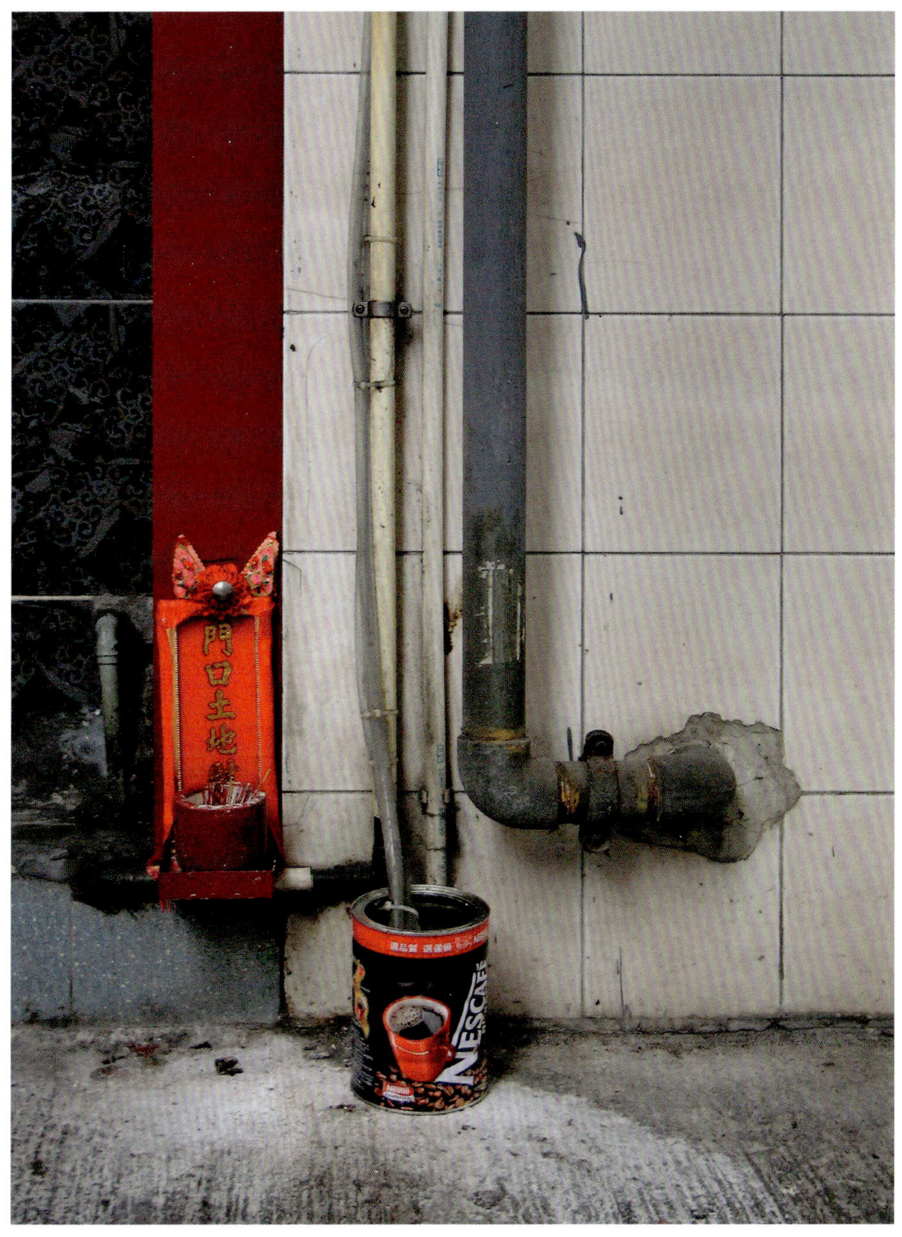
門口土地財神

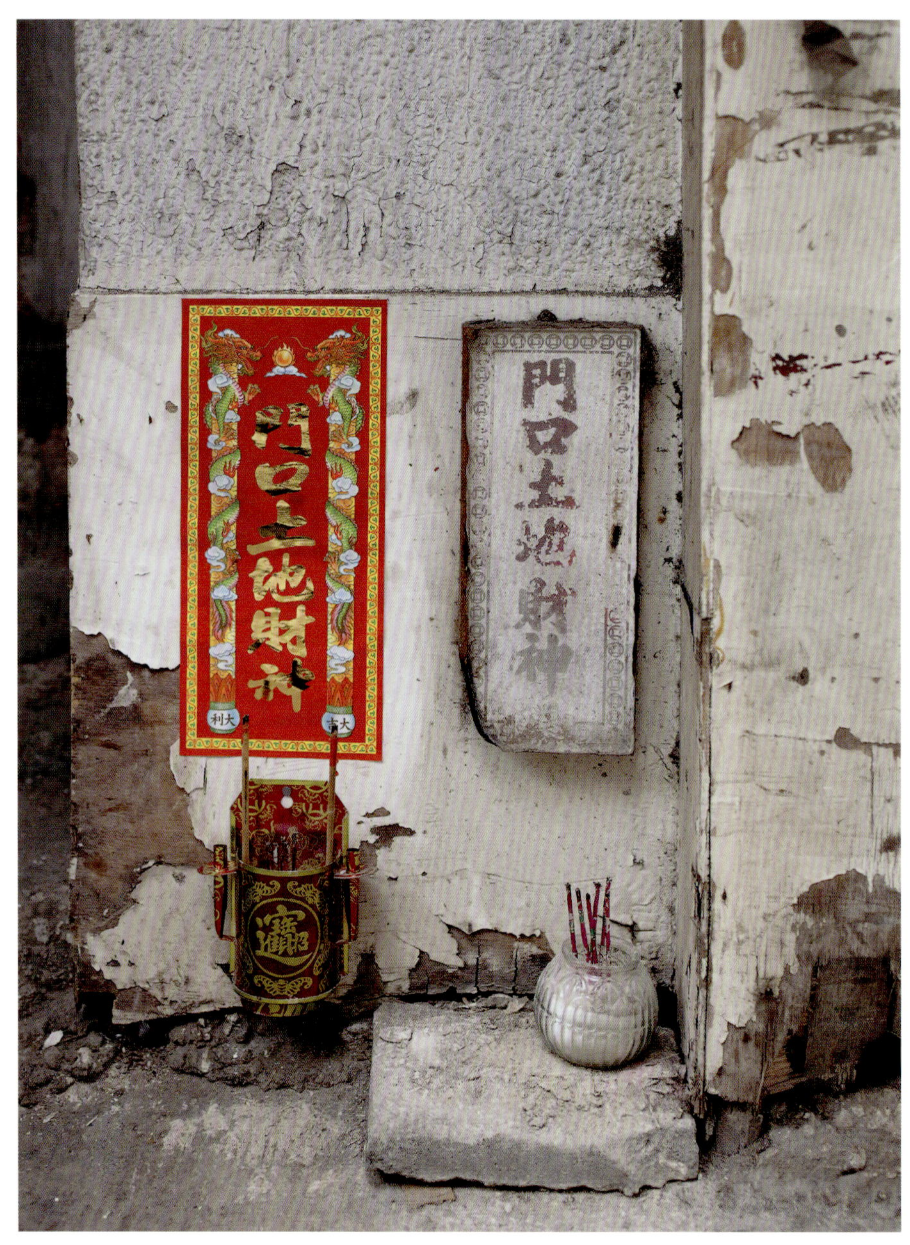

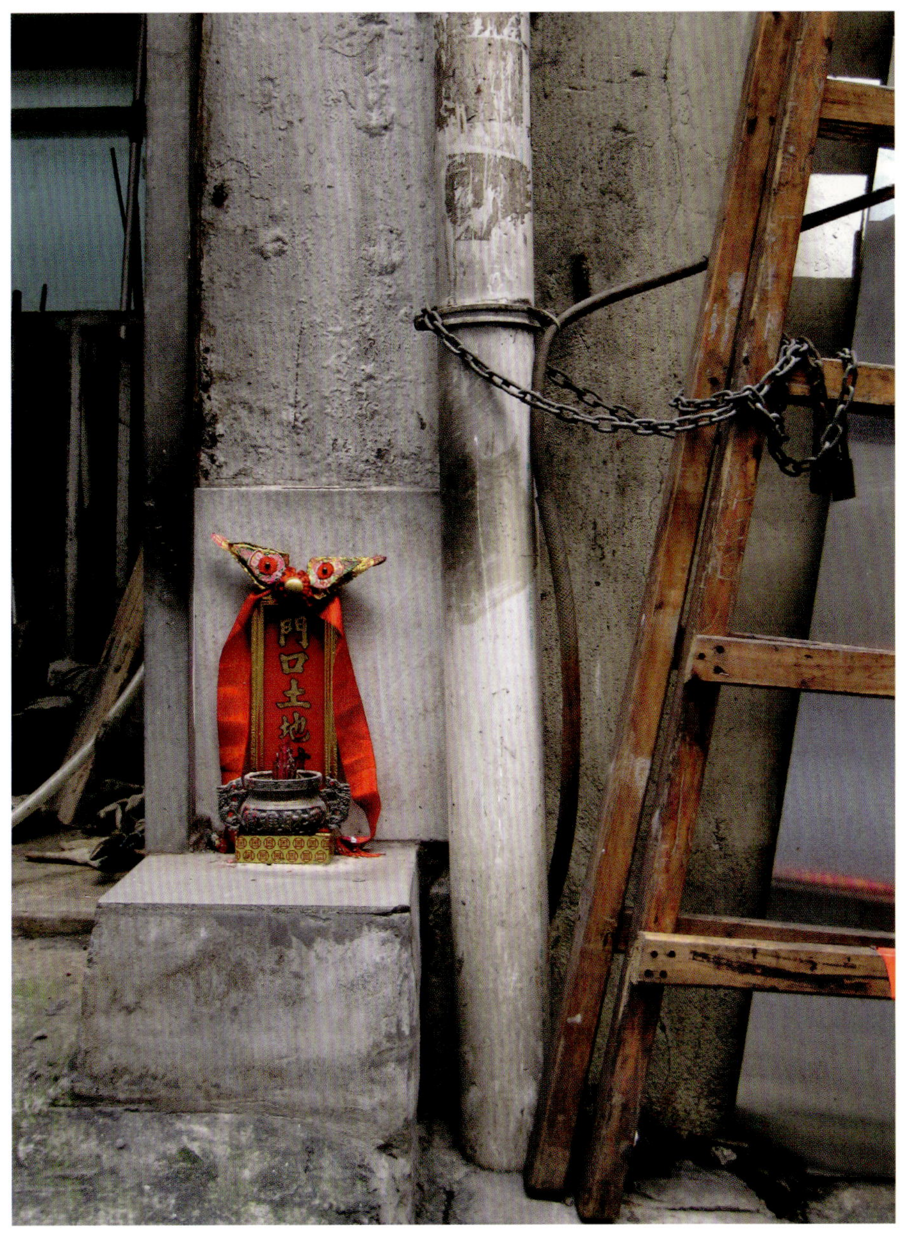

門口土地

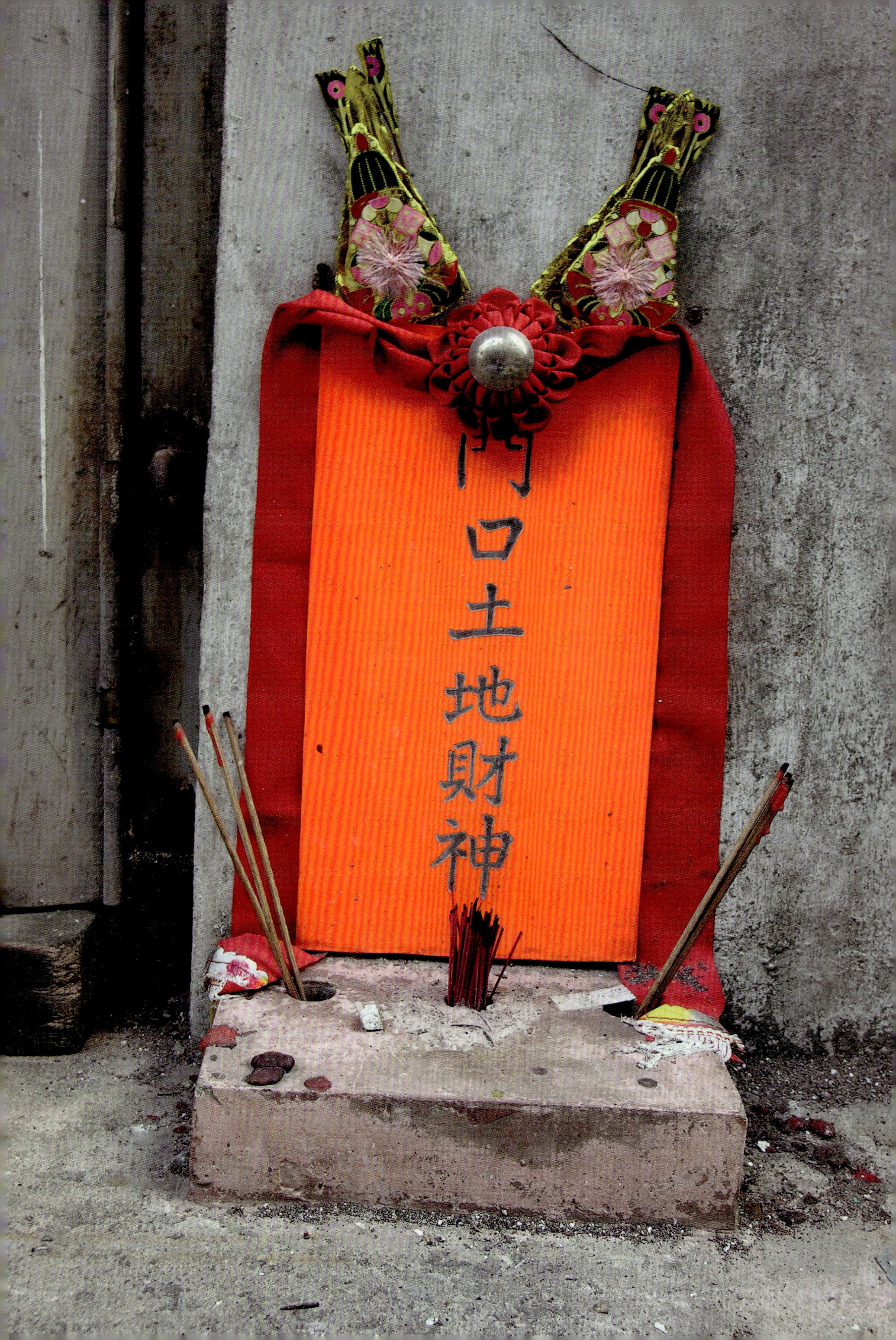

門口土地財神

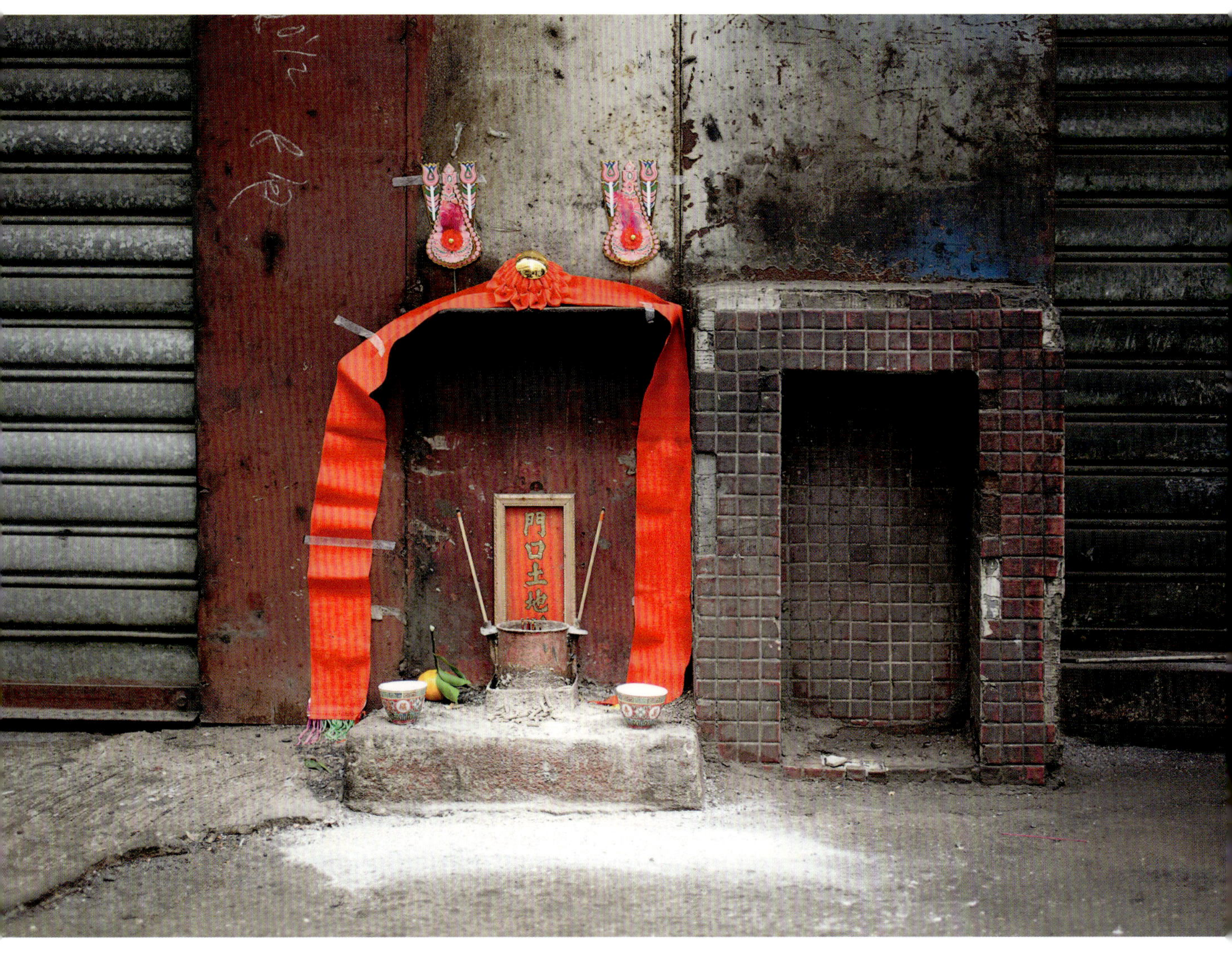

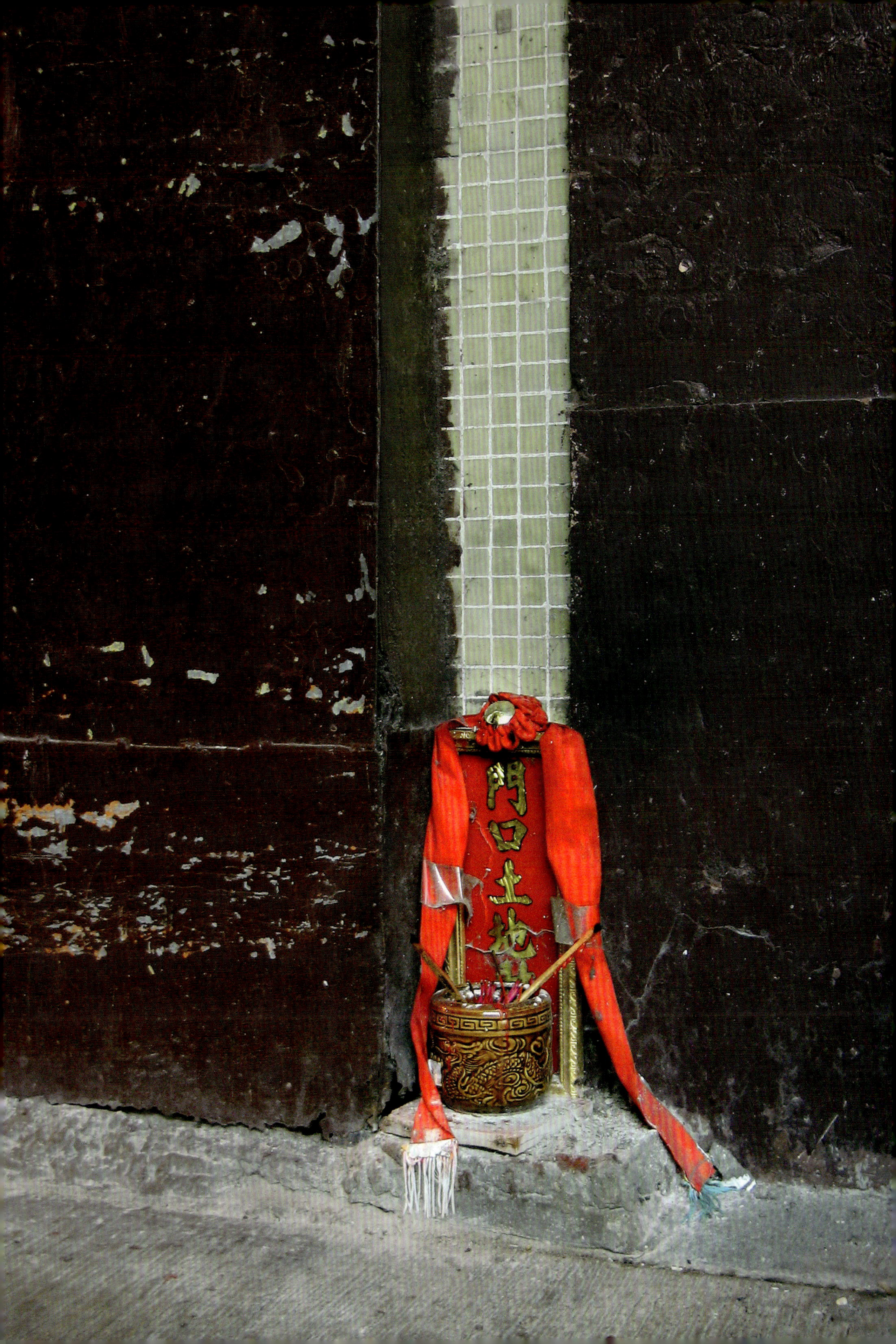

門口土地財

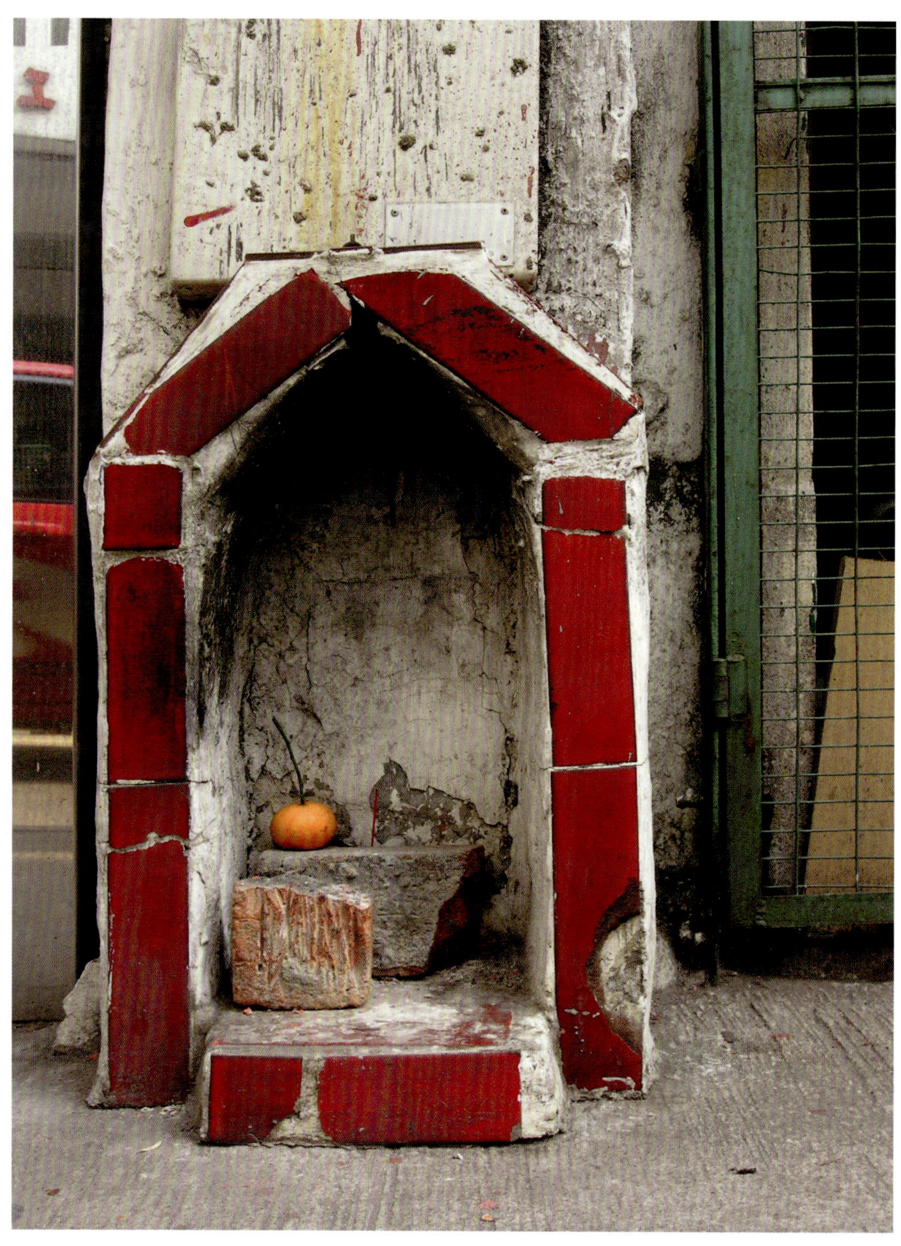

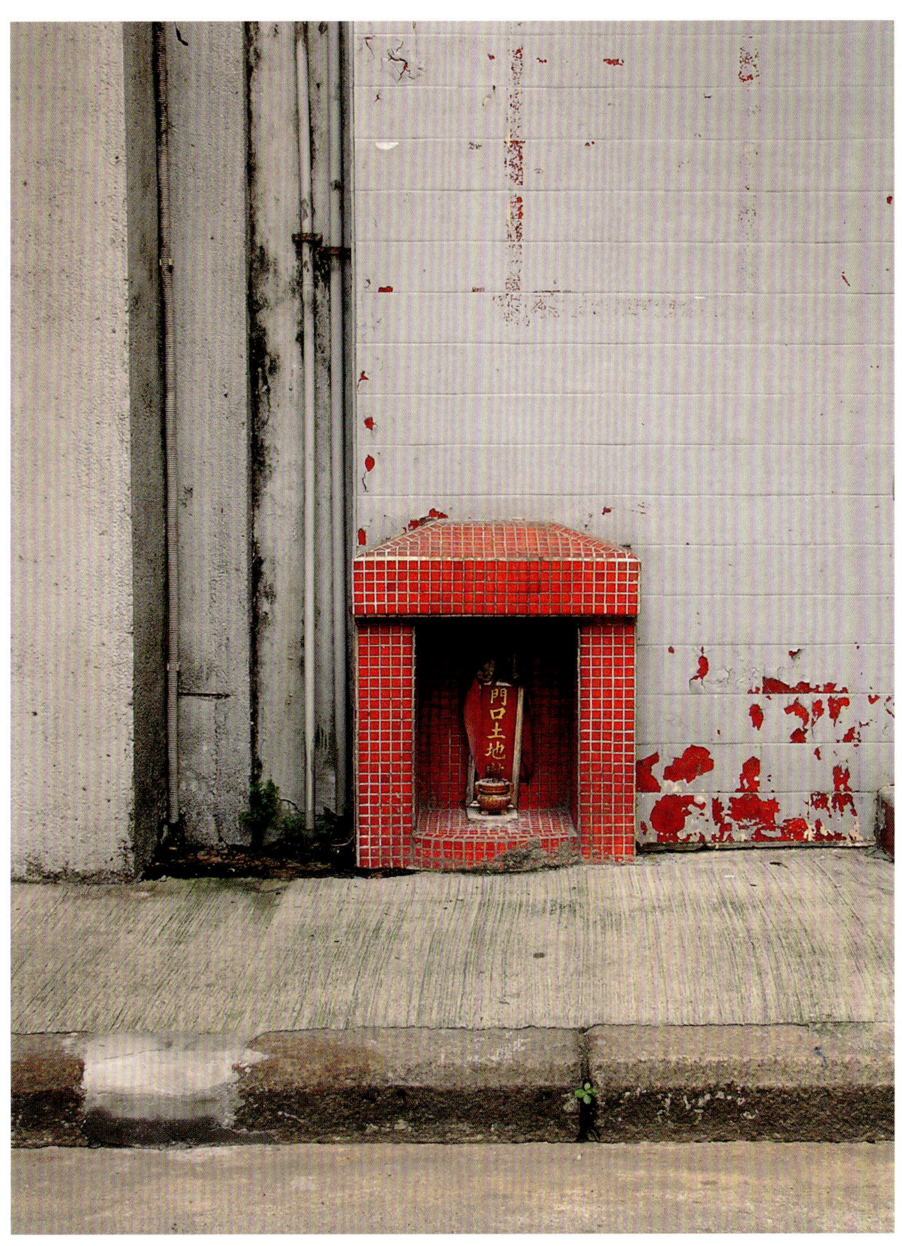
門口土地

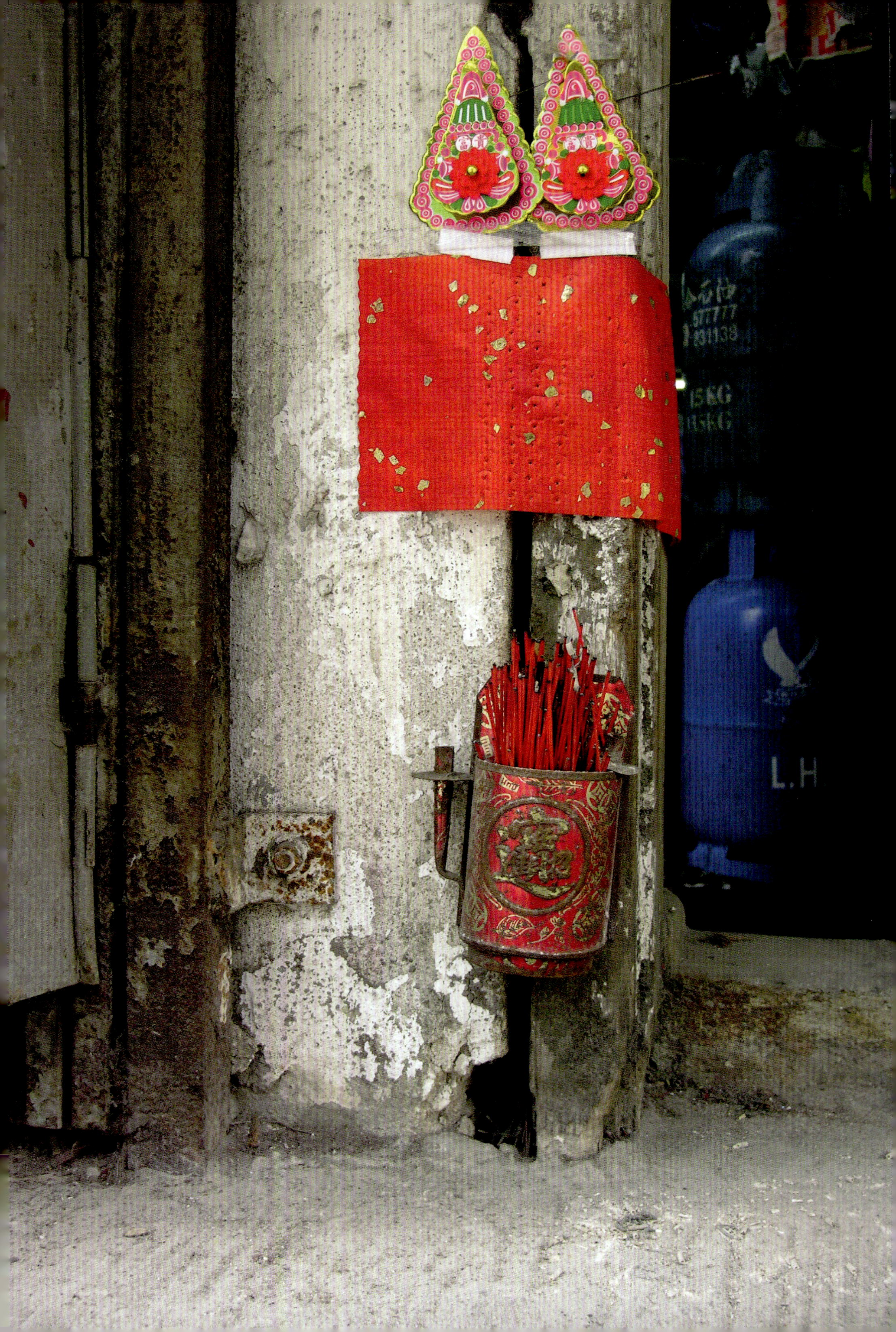

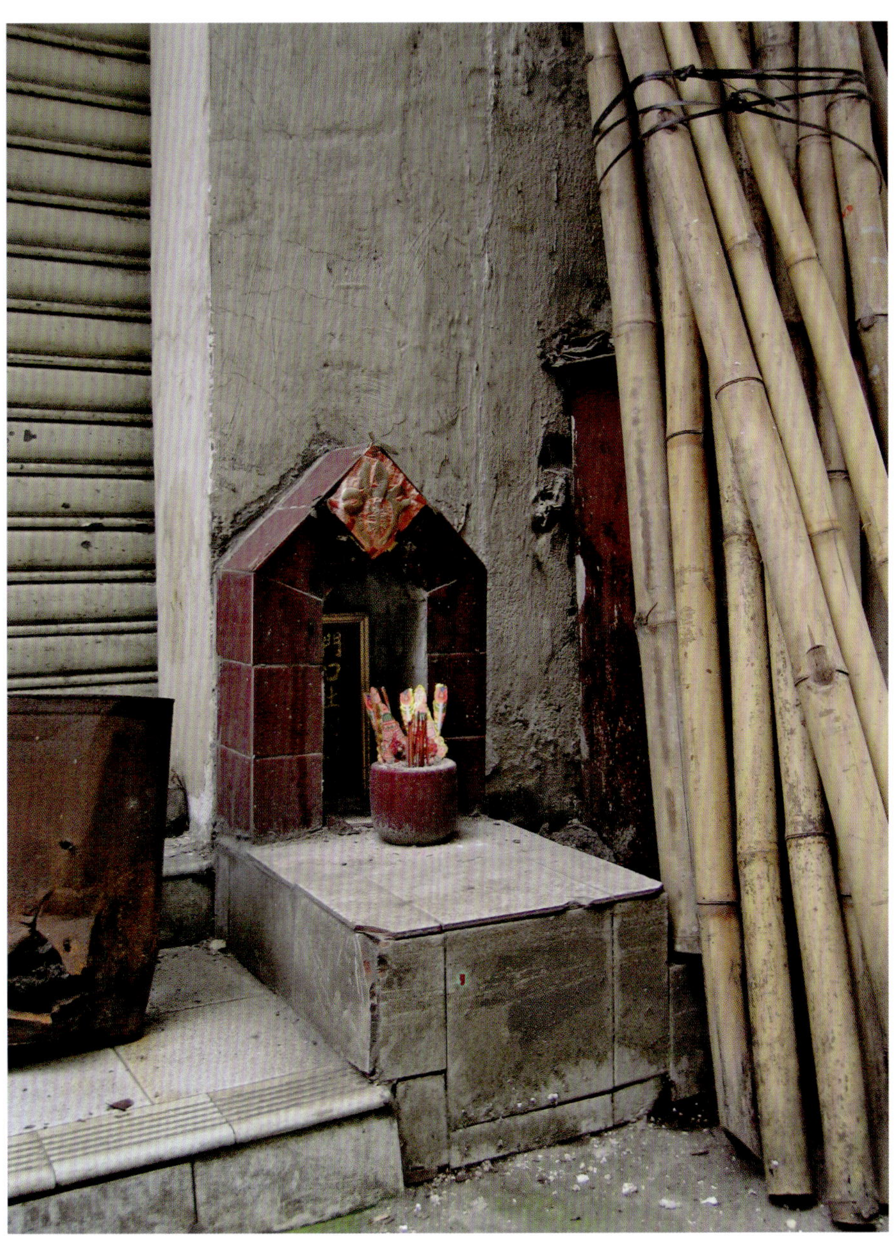

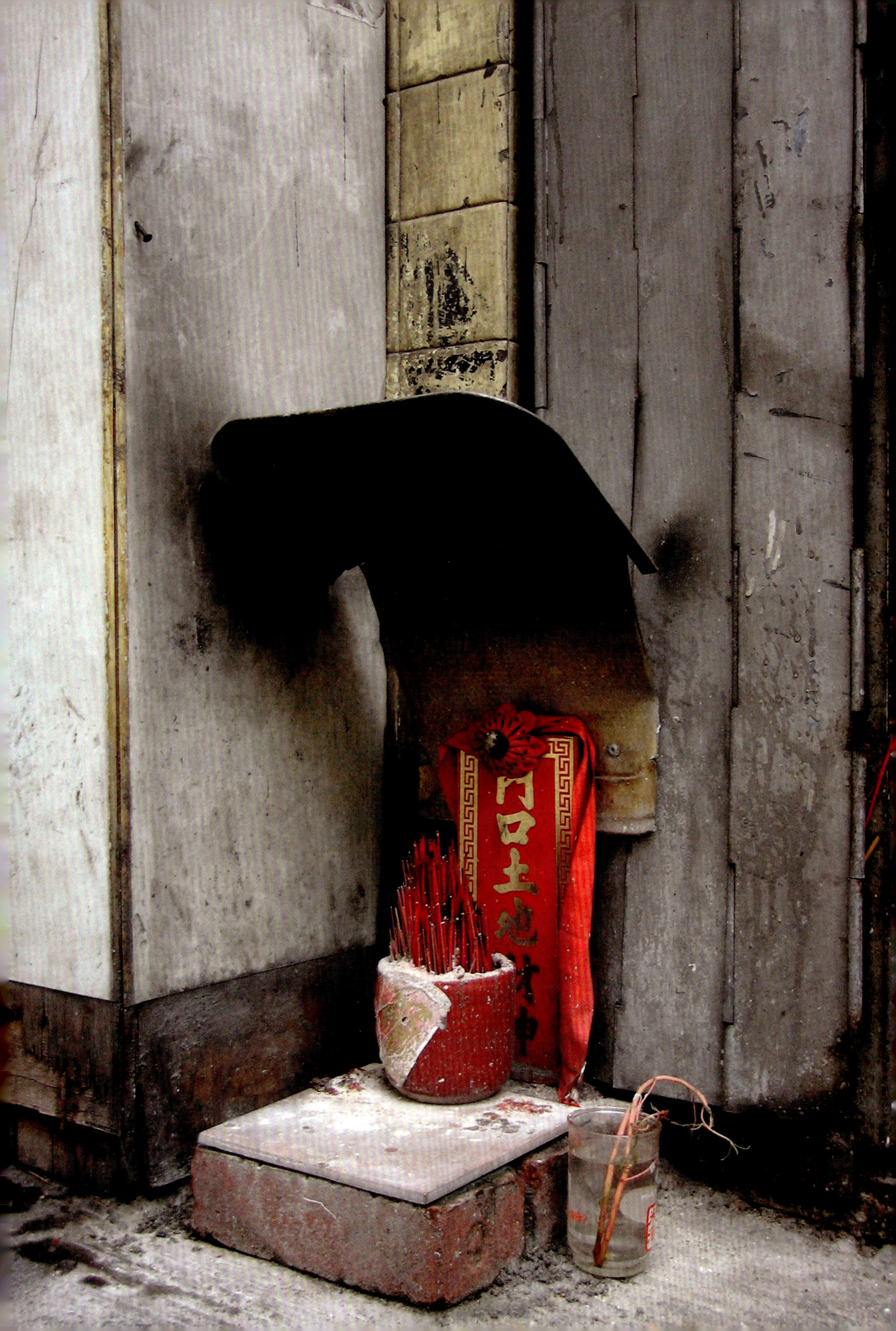
門口土地財神

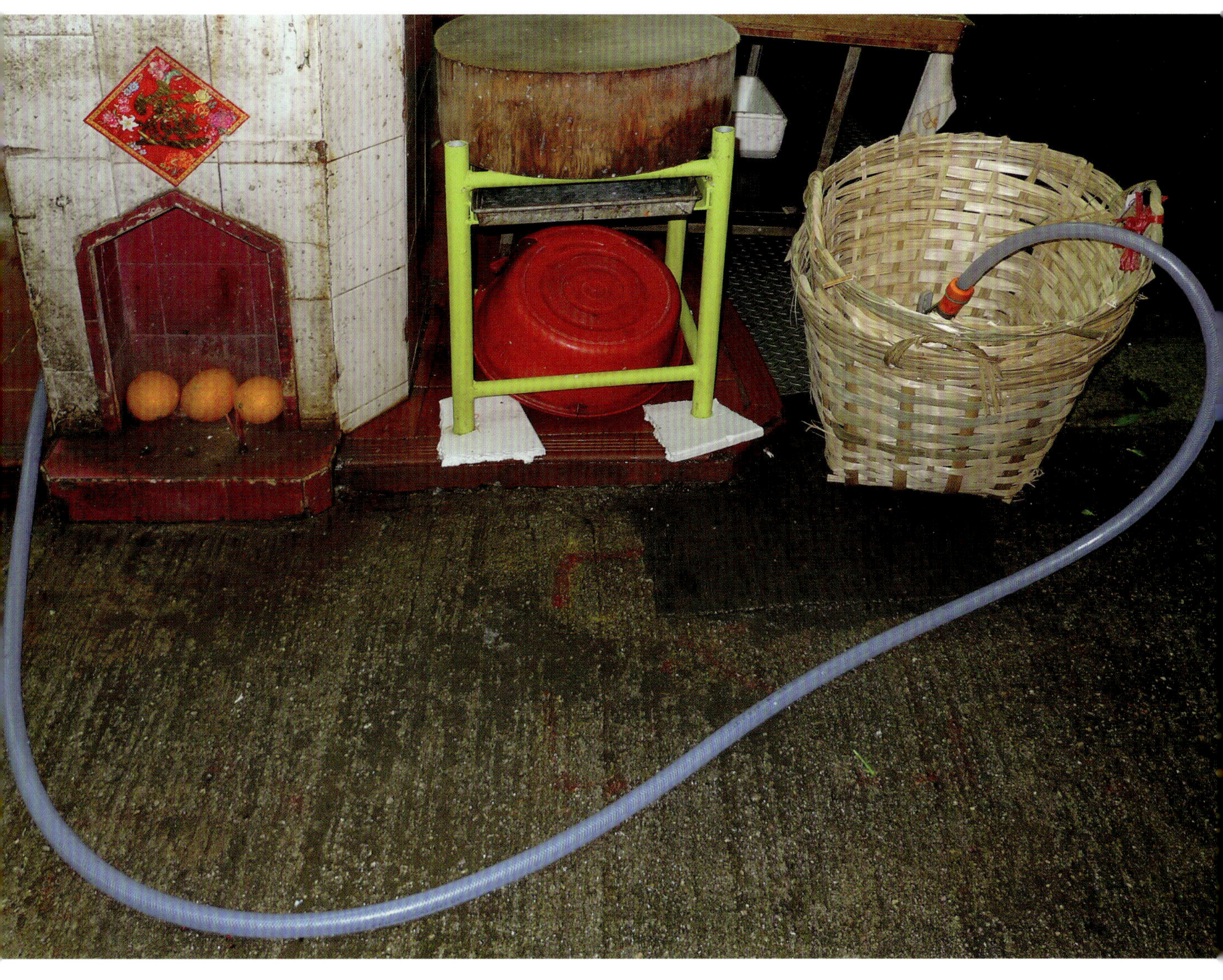

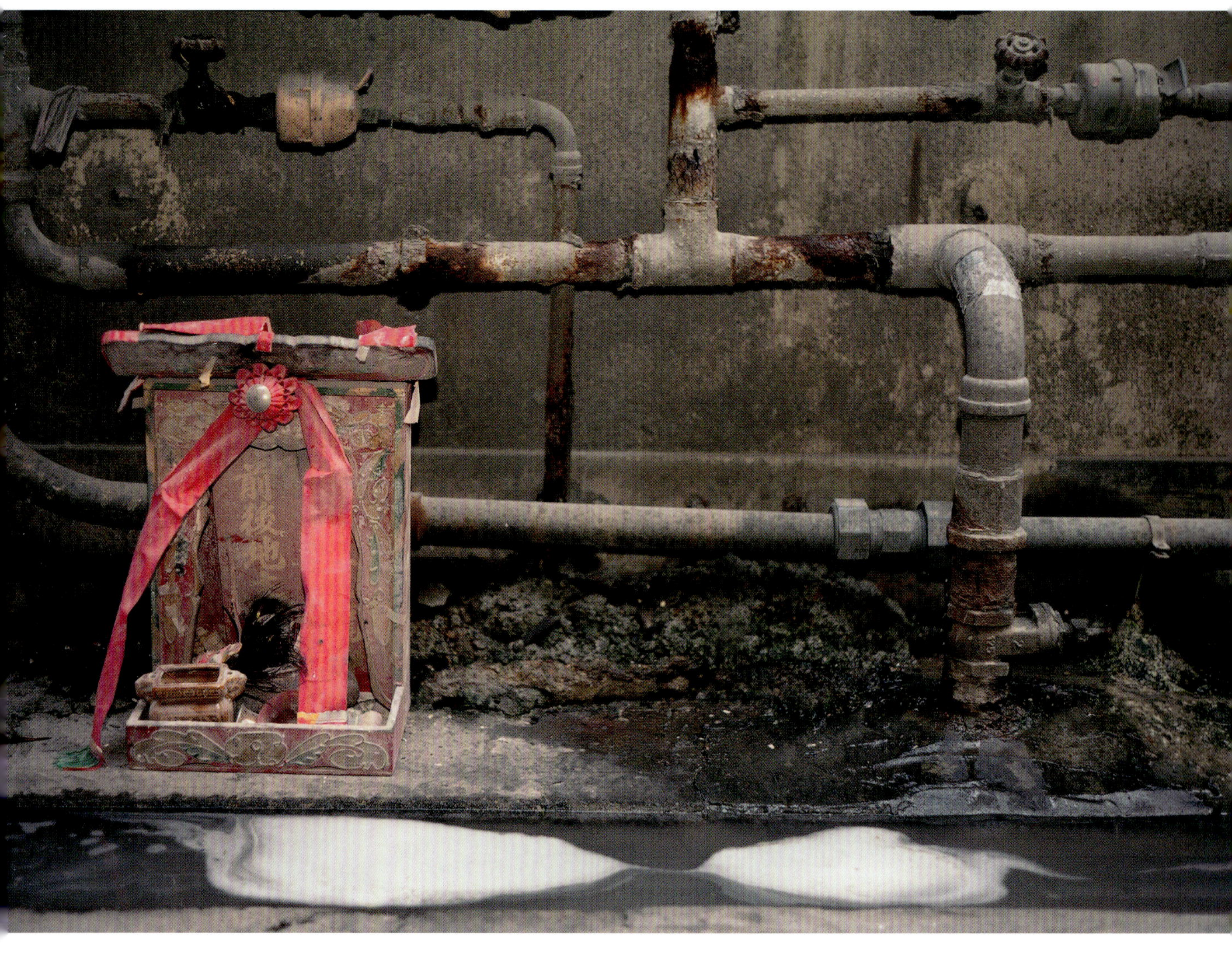

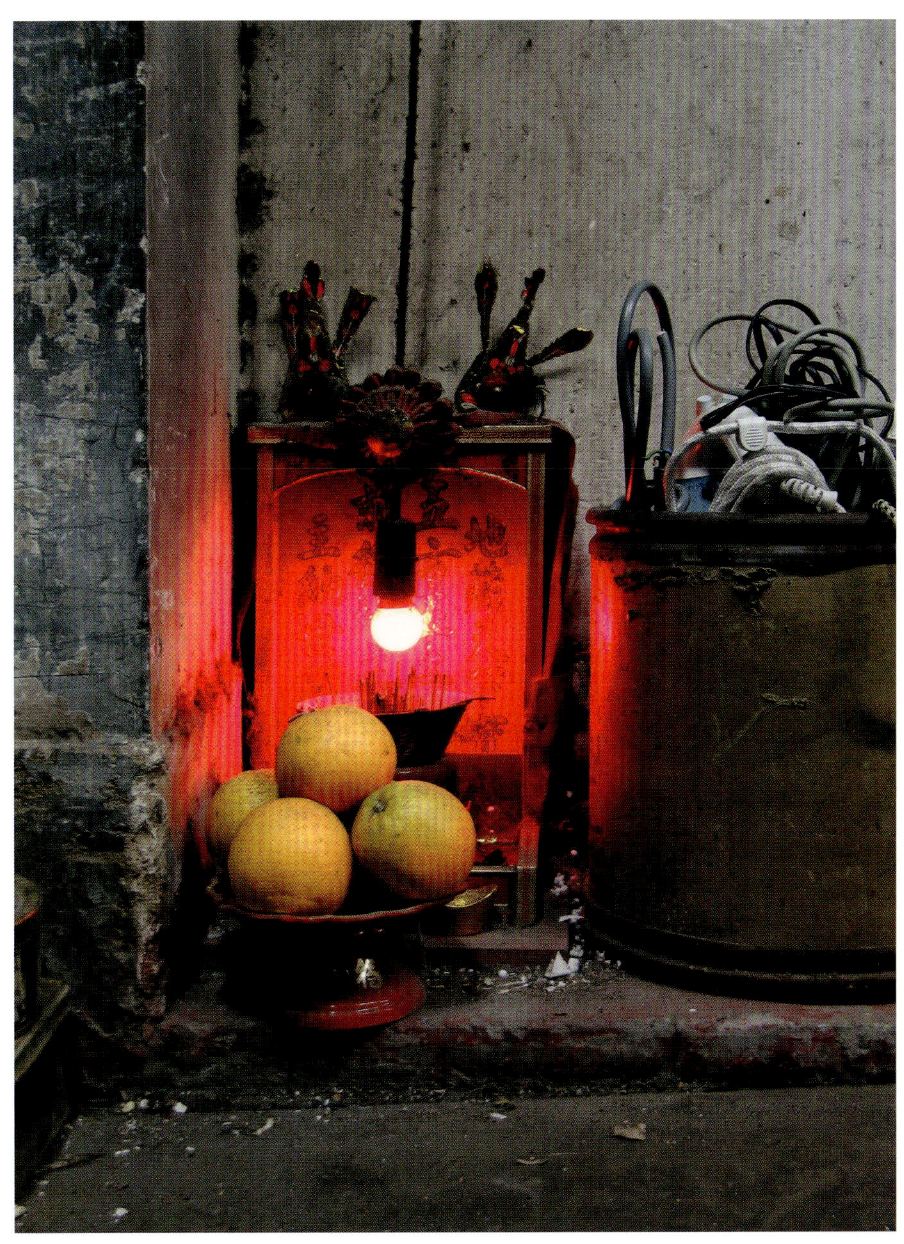

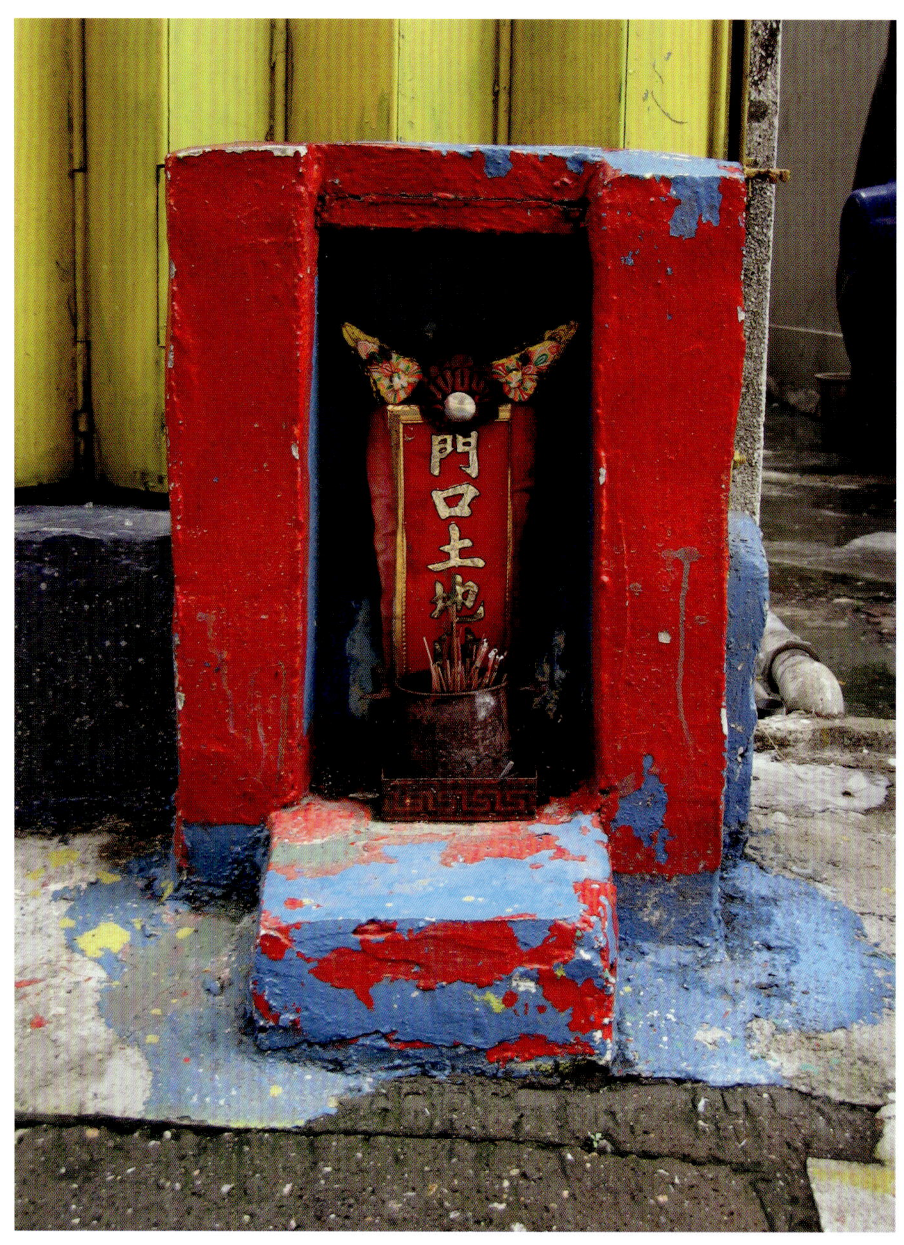
門口土地

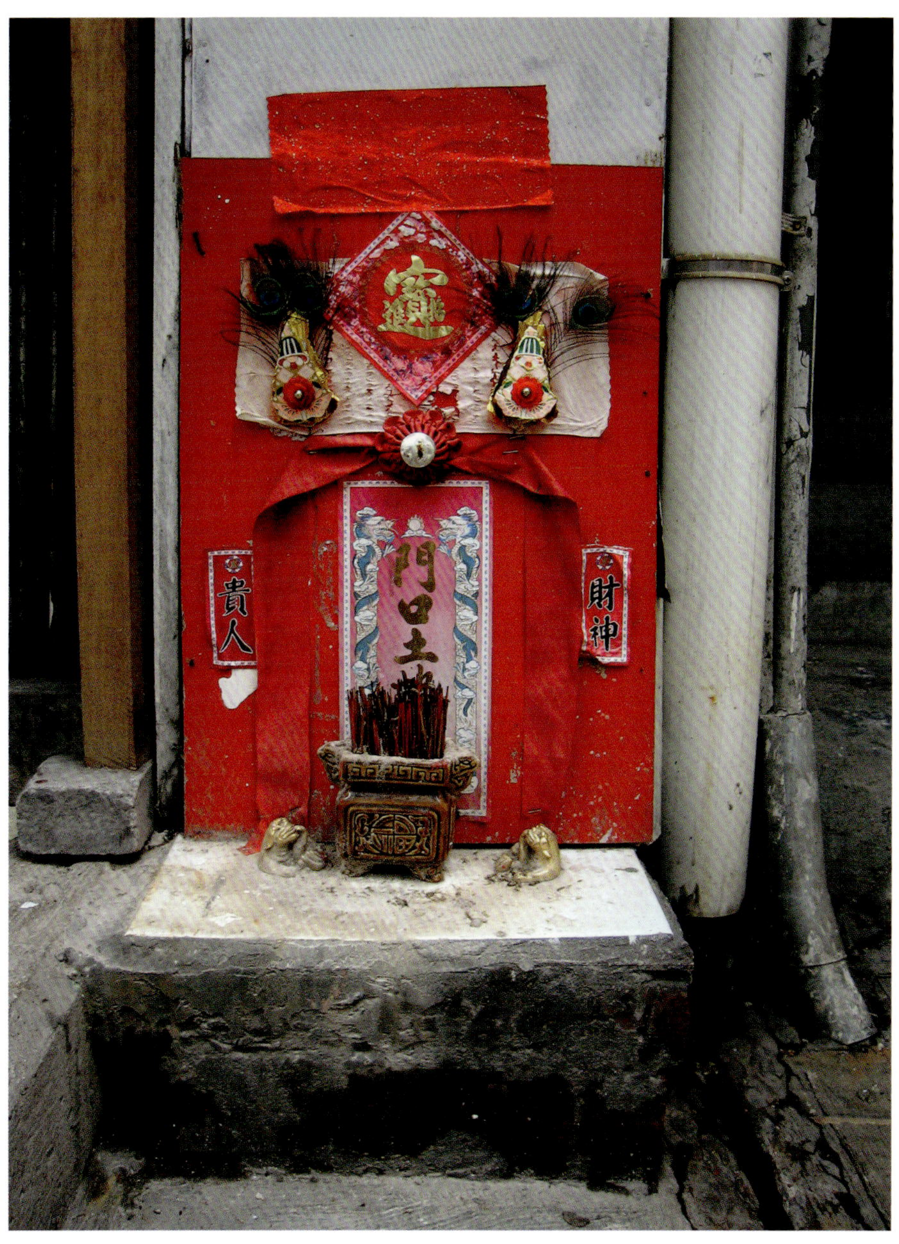

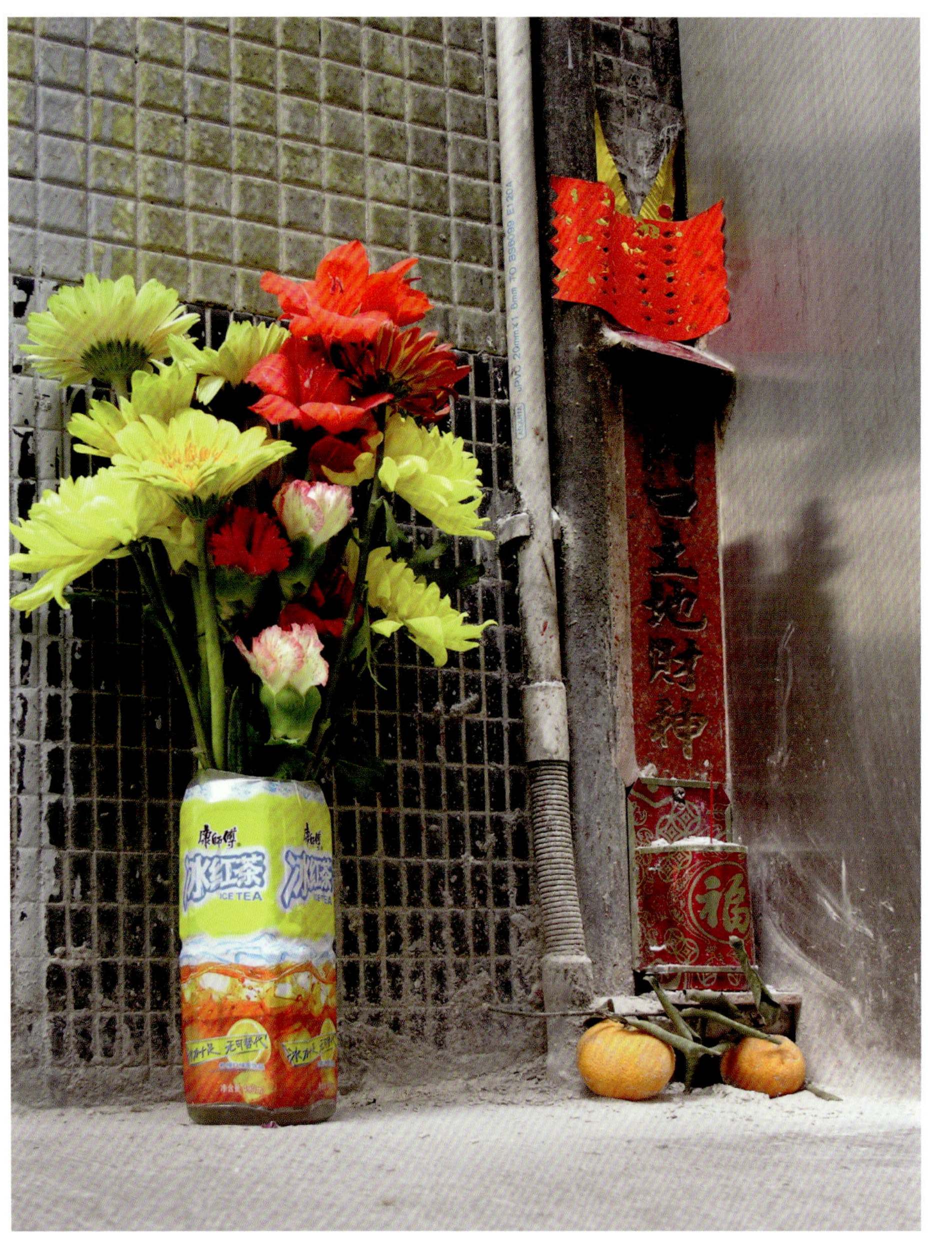

康师傅
冰红茶
ICE TEA
门口土地財神
福

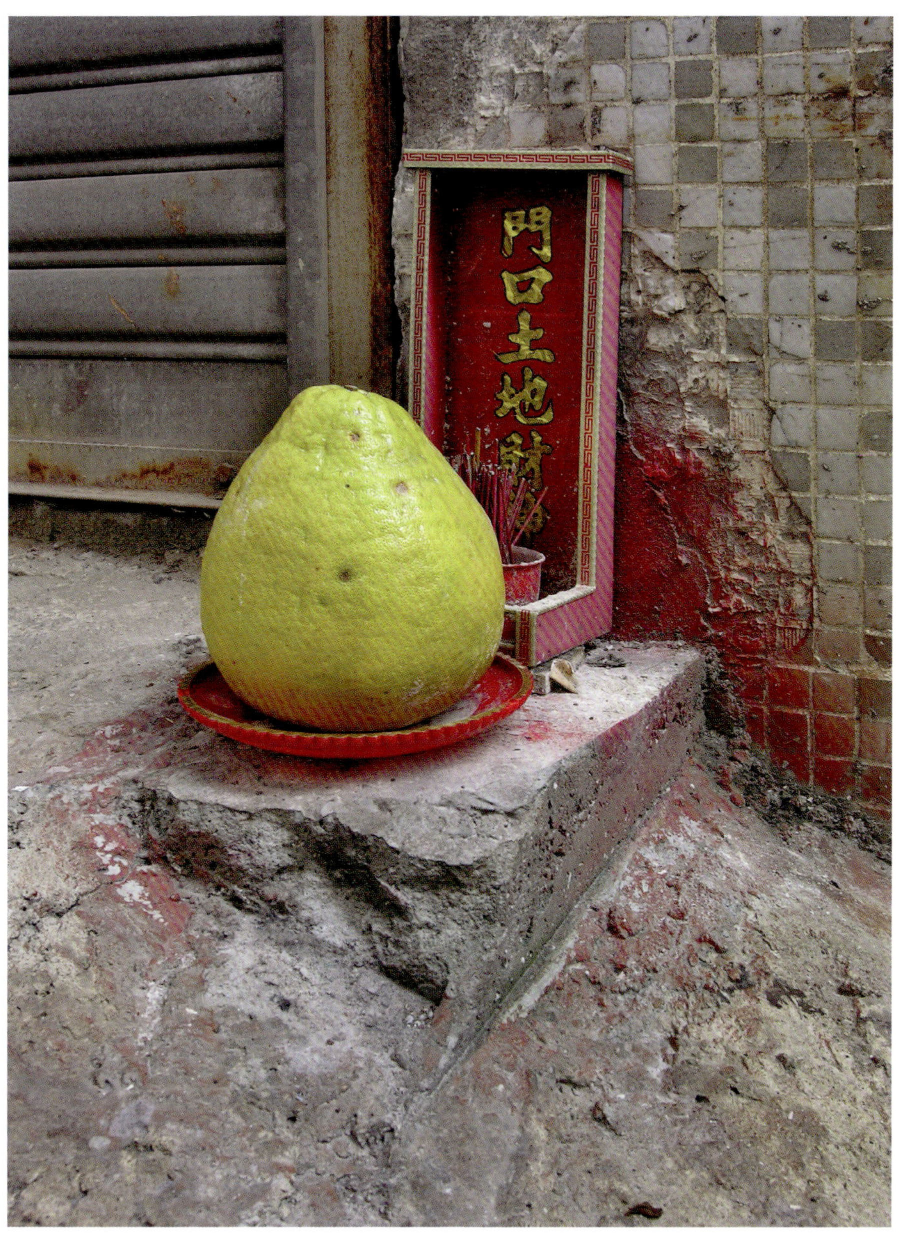

門口土地財神

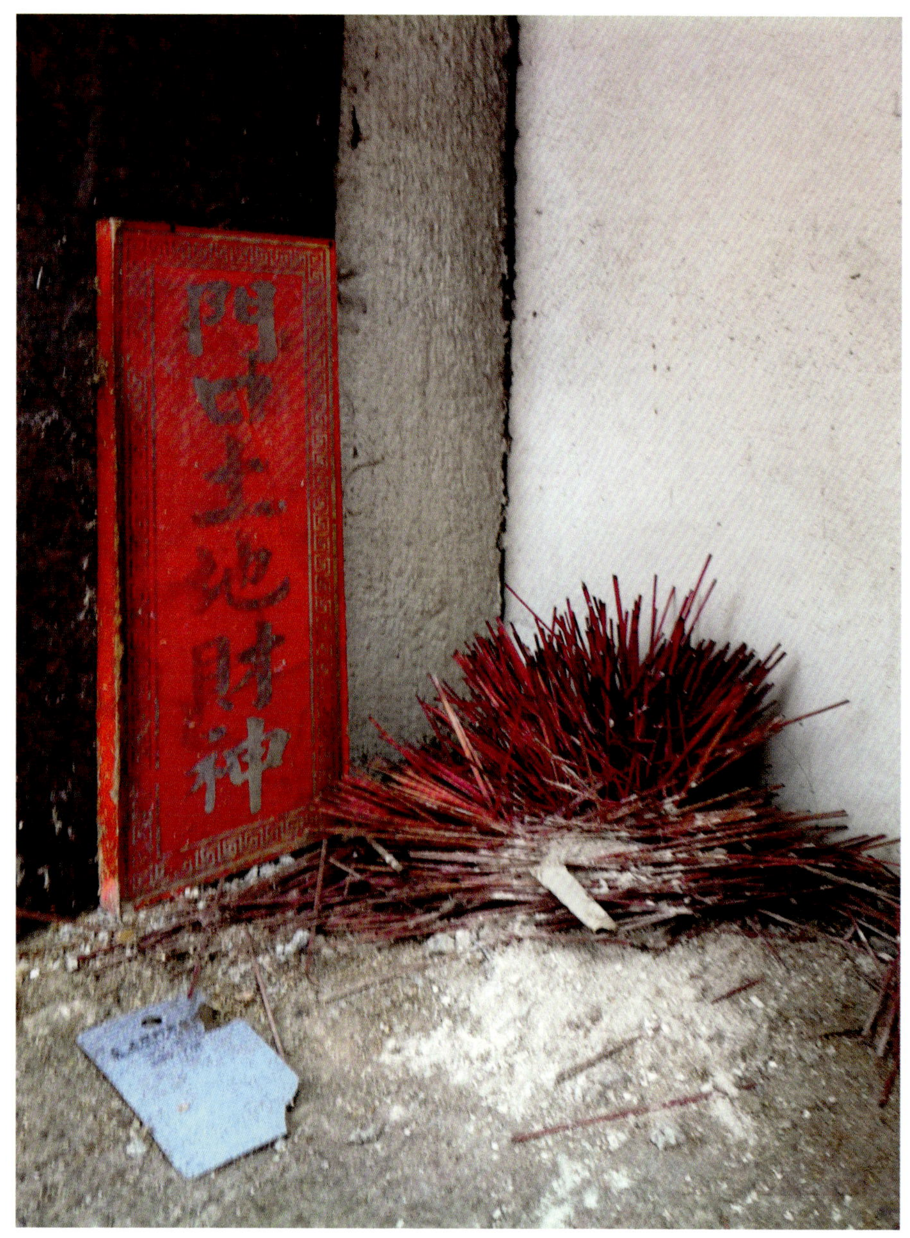

門口土地財神

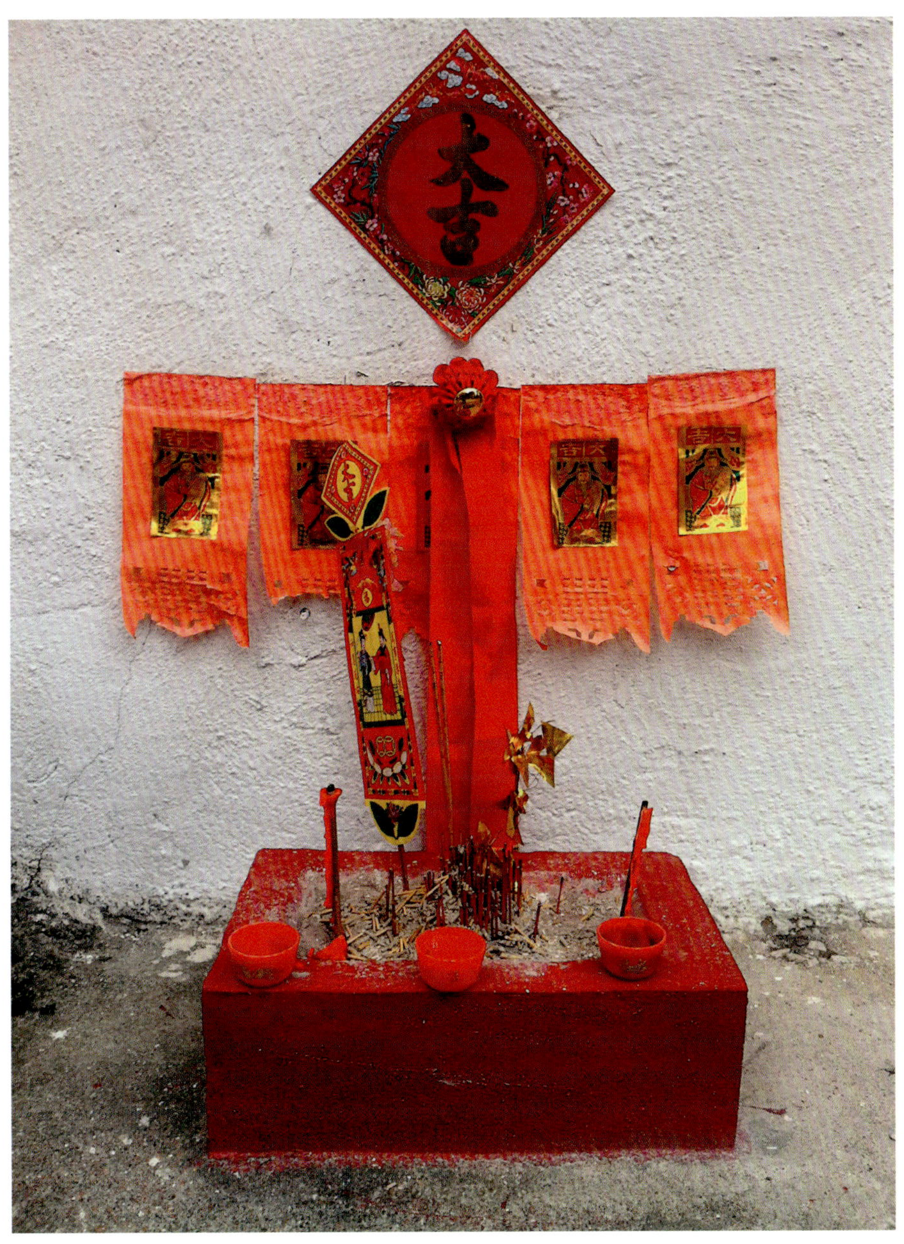

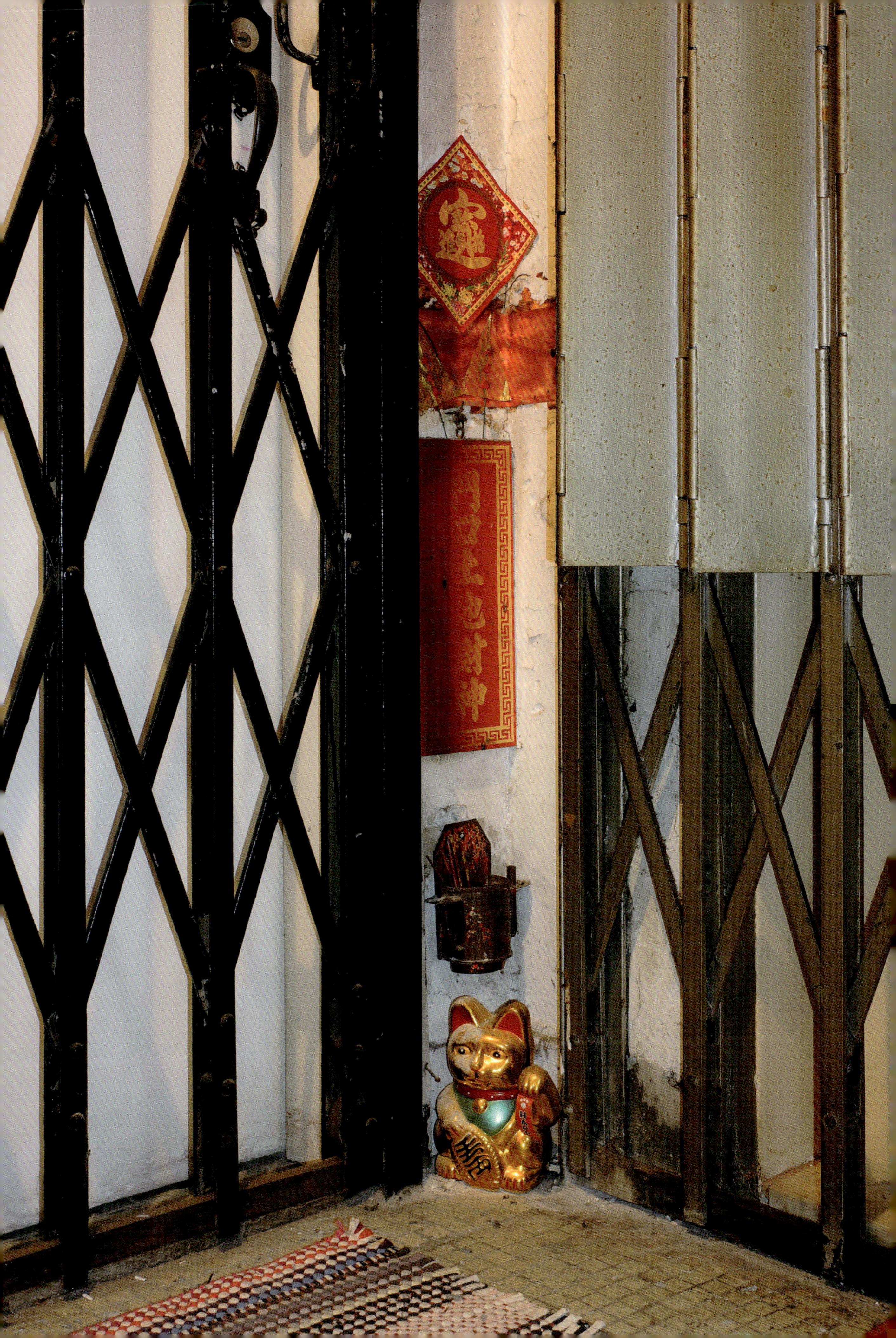

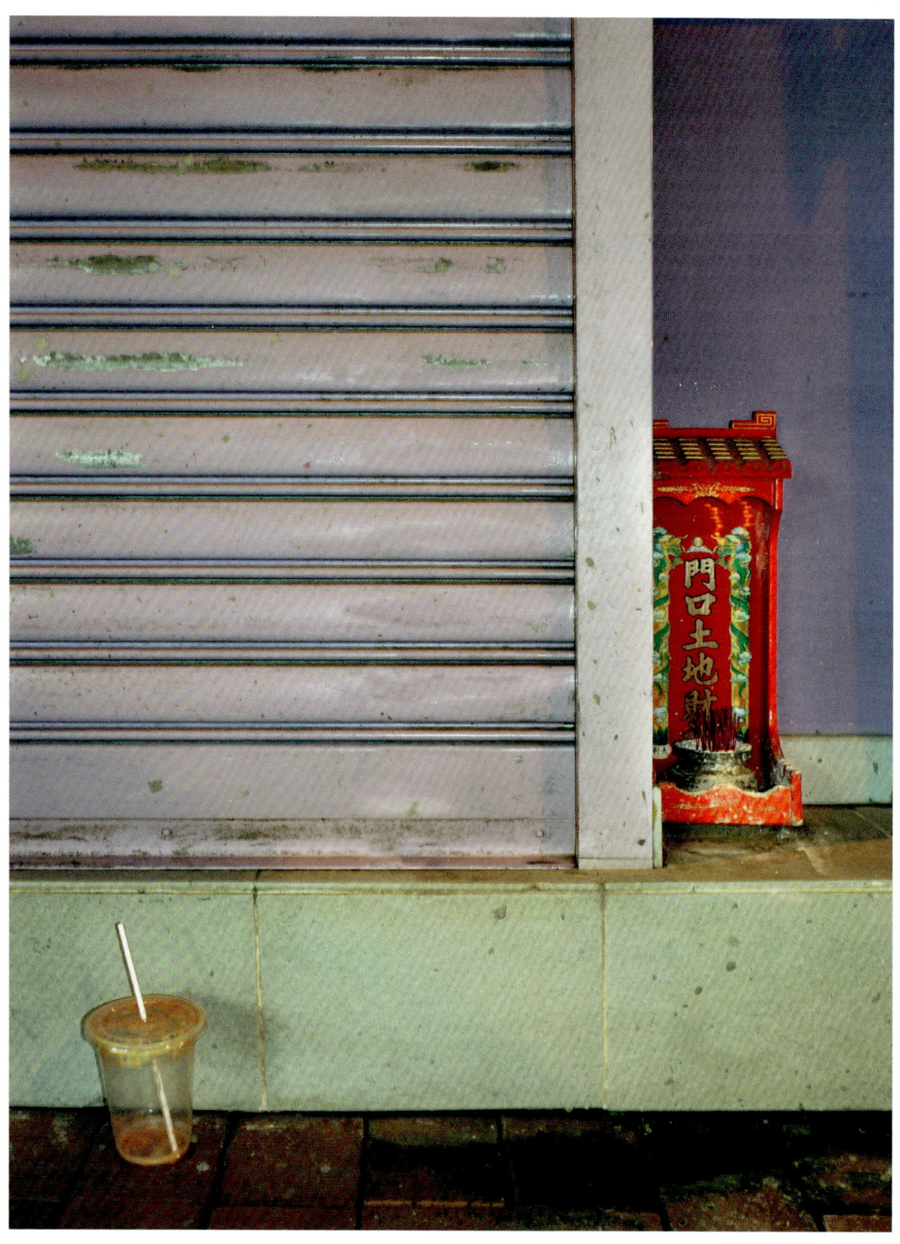

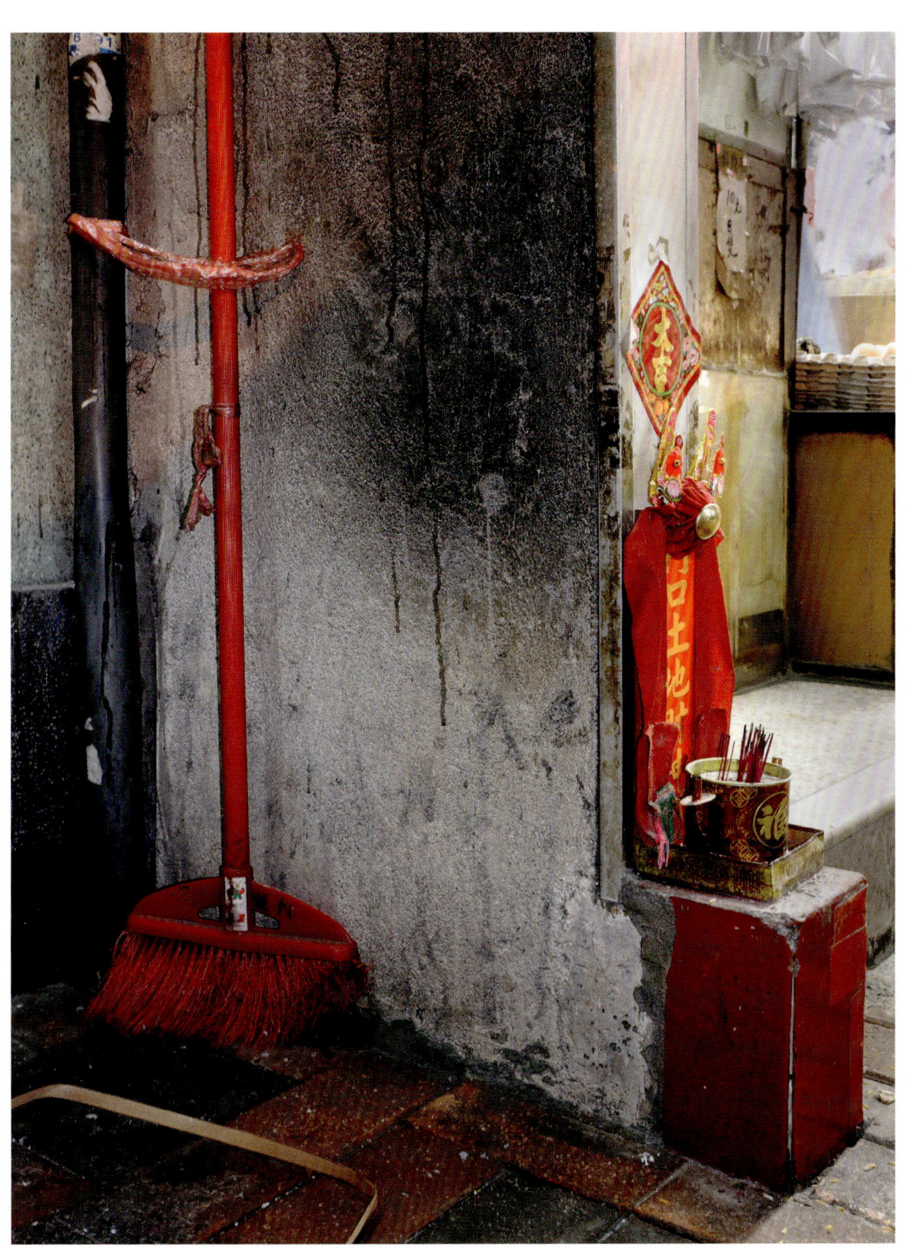

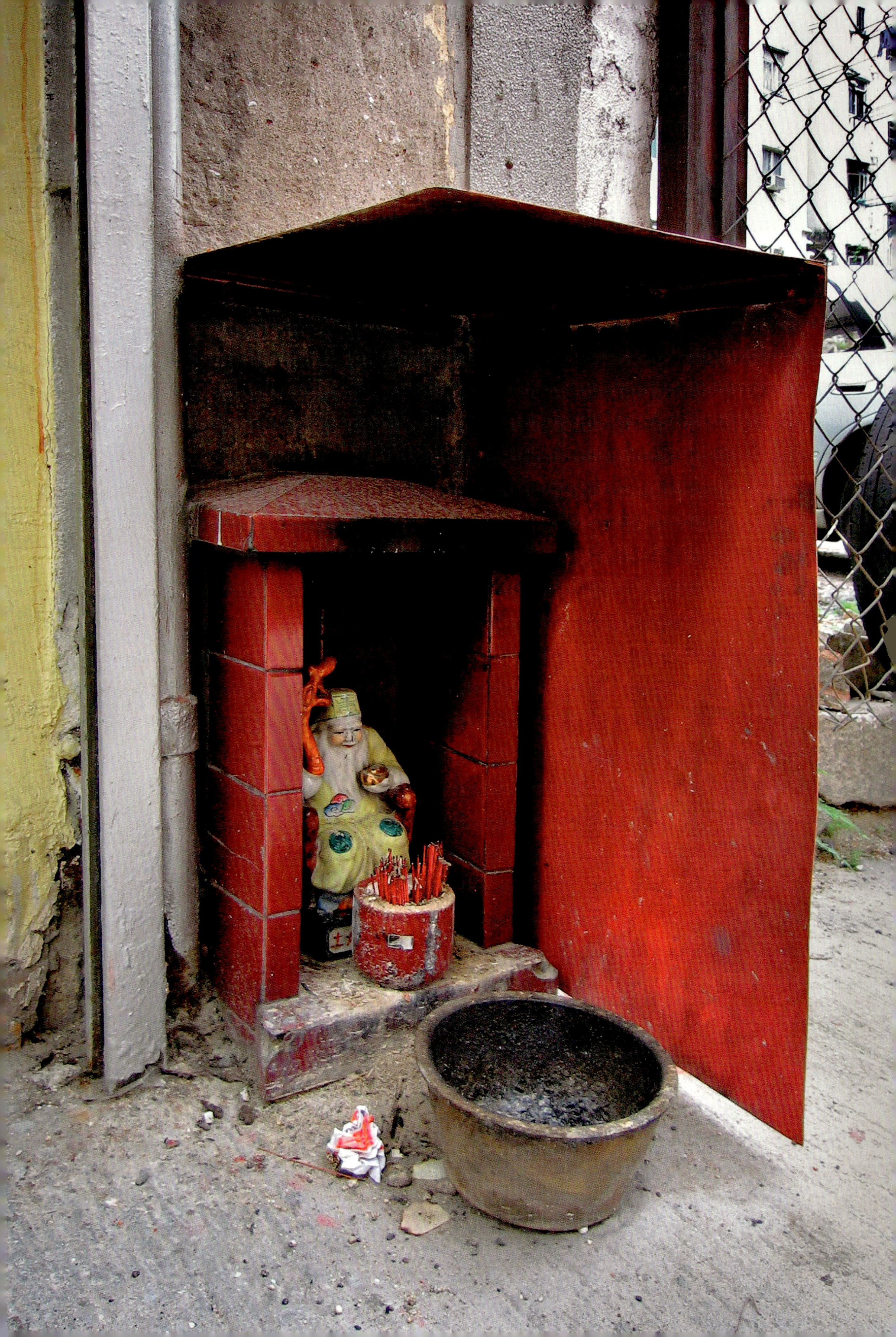

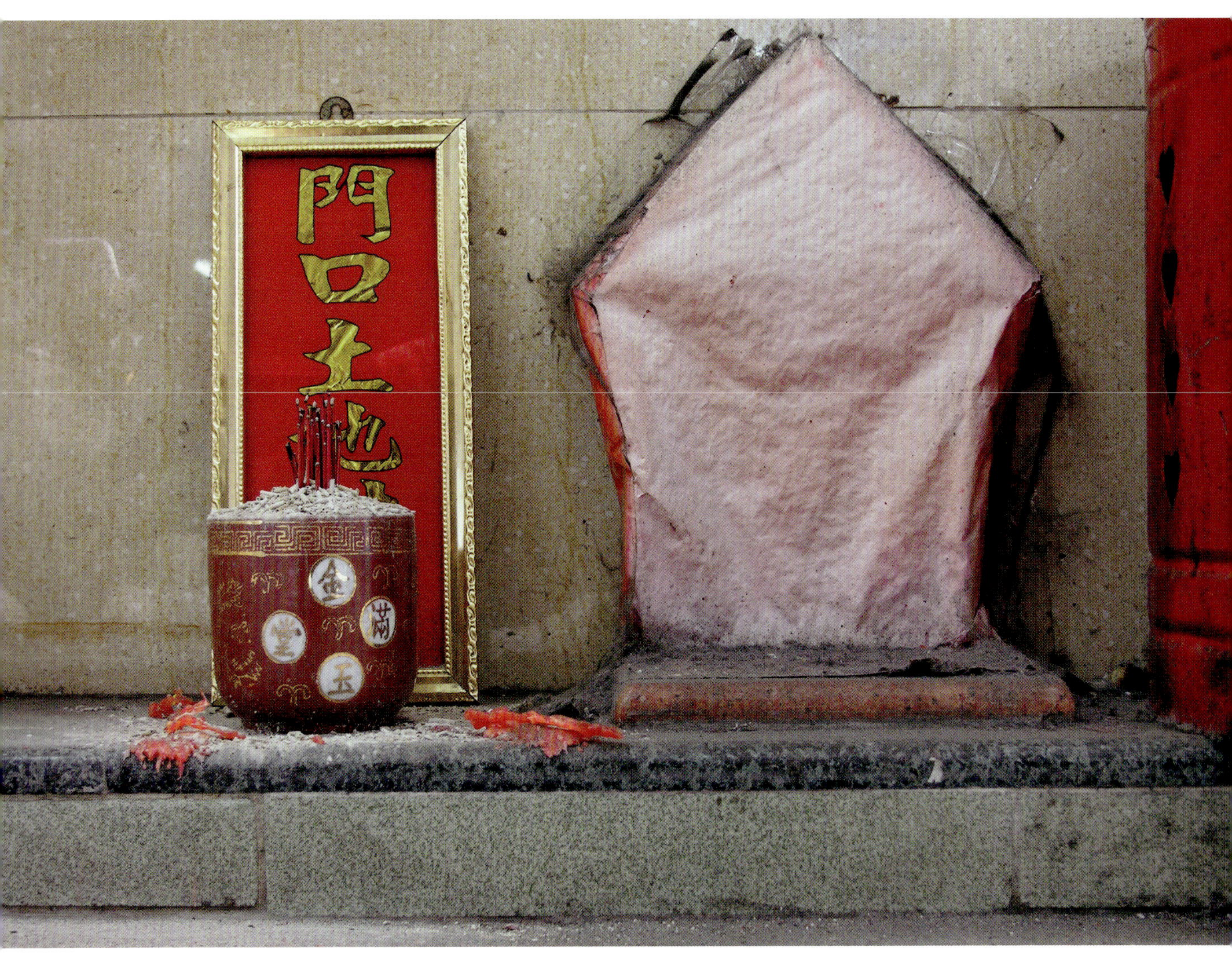

門口土地
金
滿
豐
玉

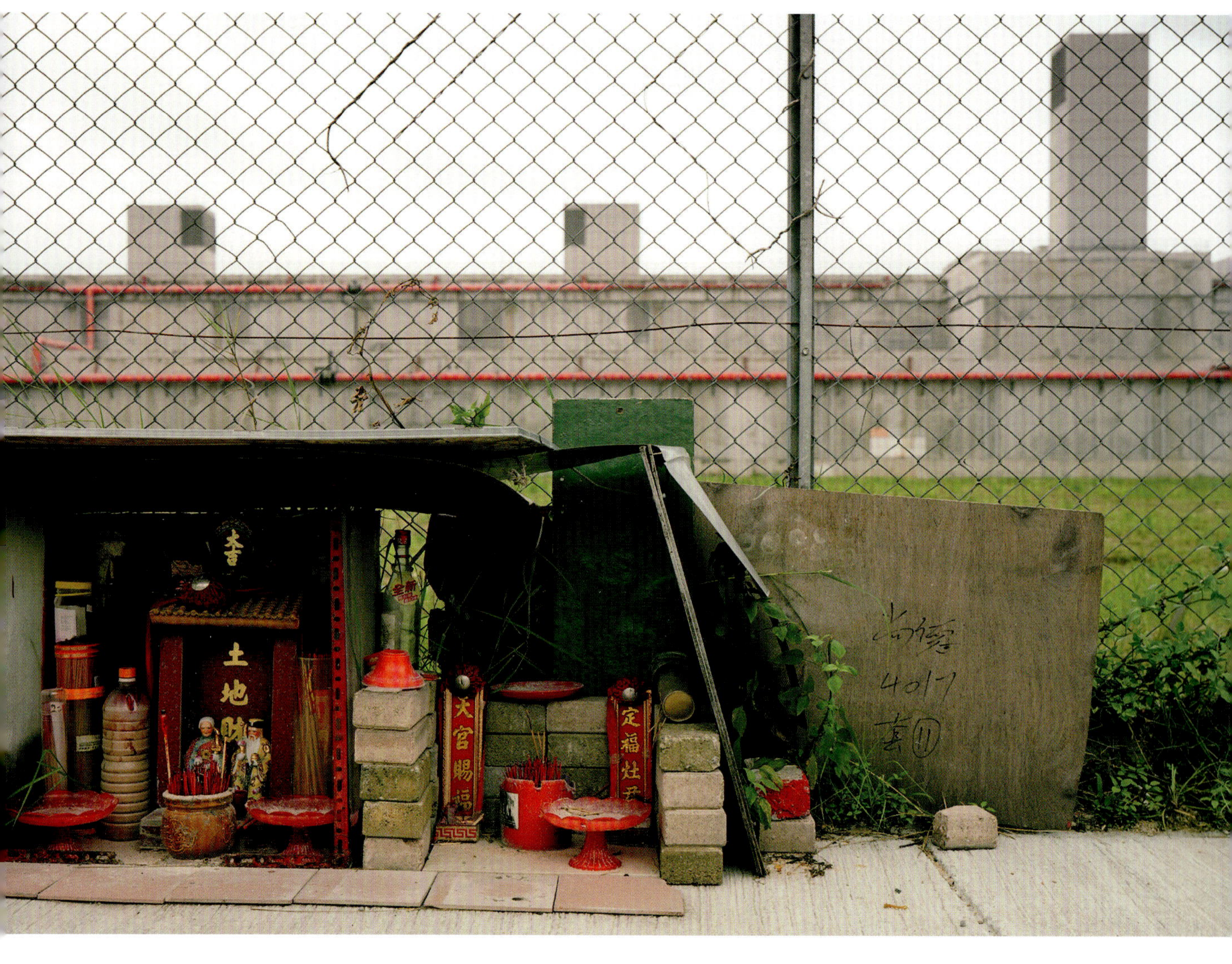

"I do believe in the Earth God. The more I worship him, the more powerful he will become," said property agent Biu Cheung, whose Earth God stands on a side street of Mong Kok.

"We give our offerings two times a day. The really devout ones will choose an auspicious time to do it, but we just worship whenever we want," he said.

Despite claiming to be "casual worshippers," Cheung and his bosses always go the extra mile to please their Earth God during festivities—while other shop owners merely offer fruits or meat, the Wai Hing Earth God is always donned in a red silk ball and decorated with golden flowers before the Lunar New Year.

"All deities fly back to heaven on the 24th day of the final month to report what they have done in the past year—just like what Hong Kong's Chief Executive does every year in Beijing," he said. "We want our Earth God to look handsome enough in front of his peers."

Before the Earth God departs on his annual voyage, he is thoroughly and meticulously cleaned with pomelo leaves soaked in water—a traditional Chinese practice to wash away all evils and bad luck.

Cheung, whose ancestors came from Chiuchow, said the Earth God was very popular there. "In Chiuchow, the Earth God is called 'Fook Tak Lo Yeh' 福德老爺 or 'Bak Gong' 伯公. Although the terminology is slightly different, their functions are similar—in charge of wealth and security in the neighbourhood."

Cheung said while all forms of businesses worship the Earth God, he understood why the deity could be more relevant to the real estate industry.

"Mainland Chinese prefer building new houses to buying second-hand flats, as they are 'spiritually clean,'" he said. "In Hong Kong, building new houses is not practical. That's where the Earth God comes into play—they shield homebuyers from ghosts and evil spirits."

He said instead of consuming the fruit offerings all by himself, the Earth God distributes them to hungry ghosts and evil spirits in the neighbourhood, so that worshippers are spared.

Having travelled a few times to Chiuchow, Cheung said he observed a number of differences between the worshipping routines.

He said villagers in Chiuchow prefer offering ducks and chickens, whereas Hong Kong worshippers mainly buy roasted pork. He added that the routines in Hong Kong are much more simplified.

"Here, it has become a natural habit to offer incense two times a day," he said. "It's almost like brushing your teeth."

The property agent said worshipping the Earth God made him feel peaceful.

"There are many inexplicable things in life," he said. "I would rather believe them to be true than not. Worshipping the Earth God does not take much time and money. Of course it's better to do it."

地產經紀張先生的店鋪，位於旺角
一條人流比較疏落的後街。

「信才會拜，拜才會靈嘛。」他説。

「我們通常每天拜兩次，虔誠的可能會
擇吉時上香，但我們則比較隨意。」
雖然張先生謙稱自己只是隨意供奉，
但惠興地產的老闆及員工都不敢怠慢。
每逢農曆新年，他們總會為土地公公
掛上金花紅球。

「每年的年廿四，所有神祇都會上
天庭匯報過去一年的功德，像特首要
到北京述職一樣。我們的土地公公
總不能在他的同伴面前失威吧。」

惠興的土地公公上天述職前，張先生
一定會先用柚子葉水把它抹乾淨，
以洗去一年積累下來的霉氣。

張先生是潮州人，他説鄉村拜土地
的習俗和香港很不同。

「潮州人叫土地做『福德老爺』或
『伯公』。雖然名稱不同，但掌管的東西
大同小異，主要保祐鄉民闔家平安、
財源滾滾來。」

雖然張先生認為所有生意人都得
依賴土地公公，但他明白為何土地公
和地產行業特別有緣。

「內地人大多喜歡建新屋或買一手
物業，因為比較『乾淨』。香港地少
人多，建新屋當然行不通，便得靠
土地公驅趕各方邪氣。」

他説土地公會將供奉的生果祭品
平均分給陰間邪靈，好使它們放過
陽界的人。張先生曾多次回鄉，
對港潮兩地的祭祀文化都有了解。

他説潮州人比較喜歡以雞鴨作供奉，
而香港人則較偏愛以燒肉。儀式方面，
繁忙的香港人通常一切從簡。

「我們早已習慣早晚各上一炷香，
像刷牙一般自然。」

張先生覺得拜祭土地公公可以安神
定心。

「世上太多不能解釋的事，寧可信
其有，不可信其無。祭祀花費不多，
但求心安理得，拜了總比沒拜好。」

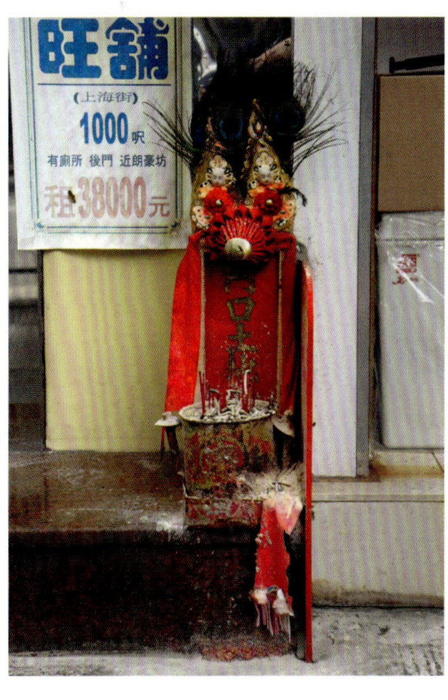

489C Shanghai Street (Soy Street corner)
Yau Ma Tei, Kowloon
九龍油麻地上海街489C號 (近豉油街街角)

Worshipper: **Ms. Winey Ip**, 50, staff member of Li Yat Kee Buddhist Utensil & Metal Wares

If the Earth God can shield shops from evil, Li Yat Kee is one of the best-protected places in Yau Ma Tei, as numerous Earth Gods are on sale here.

Shrines of different sizes—from as small as 5 inches to as large as 12 inches—greet passersby at the shopfront. Some designs are simple—just a wooden shrine inscribed with the words 門口土地財神 in golden calligraphy. Others are more lavish, made of concrete and lined with tiles, and come with colourful porcelain statues of the god.

Worshippers need to pay some HK$450 for the simple ones, and as much as nearly HK$1,000 for the larger and better-decorated ones.

"People of all ages come to shop with us," said Winey Ip, who has been a staff member of Li Yat Kee for more than a decade.

"You might be surprised that even teenagers shop here, but it's true," she said.

Li Yat Kee's very own Earth God has stood at the entrance since the shop opened more than two decades ago. Ip or her bosses worship it every morning and every evening. Like many other shops, they offer fruits to the deity during festivals.

Although the Earth God overlooks the busy Shanghai Street in the very heart of Kowloon, Ip said it has always been left in peace.

"Everyone respects it. I have worked here for more than ten years, and there has never been anyone who dares disturb the shrine in any way," she said. "Both shop owners and homeowners buy the Earth Gods," she said. "It's a traditional Chinese custom."

Although the shrines come in different sizes and designs, Ip said it is difficult to tell which is the most popular product. "People buy the shrines according to the conditions of their shops or homes."

While other gods are also on sale in the shop, Ip said the Earth God is the most down-to-earth one. "Guan Di represents righteousness and protects all businesses. Guan Yin represents benevolence and protects temples. The Earth God, on the other hand, protects all houses, including shops and homes."

But she said there is no such thing as the "most popular deity," as people choose their own gods based on personal preference and desire.

She said the shop's customers are not merely residents from the neighbourhood. "Many people come all the way from Singapore, the States, Malaysia and Thailand. They are Overseas Chinese who want to continue worshipping, but cannot find similar shops where they live."

Ip said she personally did not quite believe that the Earth God had special powers, but agreed that everyone needs peace of mind. "All Chinese people should respect this custom," she said.

如果土地公公確能保平安，相信售賣
土地神位的李日記必定是油麻地其中
一處最安全的地方。

形形色色、大大小小的神位，通通都能
在這兒找到。由最小的五吋到最大
的十二吋，豐儉由人。有些設計較簡單，
只在紅木上刻有「門口土地財神」
六個金字。有些設計則較華麗，以瓷磚
鋪面，並附有神像。

最便宜的神位，四百五十元已有交易，
而最貴的定價則接近一千元。

葉女士在李日記已工作了十多年，認識
不少熟客。

「我們的顧客，甚麼年紀都有。你可能
不會相信，但有好些熟客只有十多歲！」

李日記自己的土地公公，早於二十多
年前開業時就已屹立在入口處。員工
早晚上香，初一、十五的時候，則會
奉上水果。

雖然上海街車水馬龍、人流暢旺，
但葉女士說從來無人敢打擾土地公公。
「我已經在這裡十幾年了。多年來
人人都尊敬它，從沒有人肆意破壞。」

「無論是店東或業主都會買土地公公，
這是中國人的習俗。」

李日記的土地神位種類繁多，但葉女士
說很難斷定哪一個尺寸最受歡迎。

「宗教用品通常比較個人化，大家根據
家中或店鋪大小購買合適的神位，所以
沒有一款特別多人買。」

葉女士繼續說，土地公公算是眾神中
最親近所有人的一位。「關帝代表正氣，
掌管生意，觀音則象徵仁慈，專門保祐
佛堂。而土地呢，它保祐所有房屋，
包括店鋪和住宅。」

其實沒有一位神祇是特別受歡迎的，
人們都是按其需求而選擇安設甚麼神
祇的。

除了附近的街坊會到店裡買祭祀
用品外，也有來自五湖四海的客人。

「很多人專程由新加坡、美國、
馬來西亞、泰國等地到來。他們主要
是華僑，想繼續傳統習俗卻沒法
在當地買到合適的用品。」

葉女士說她個人不太相信土地公公
很「靈」，認為拜祭只為求安心。「這是
中國人的傳統習俗，值得尊重。」

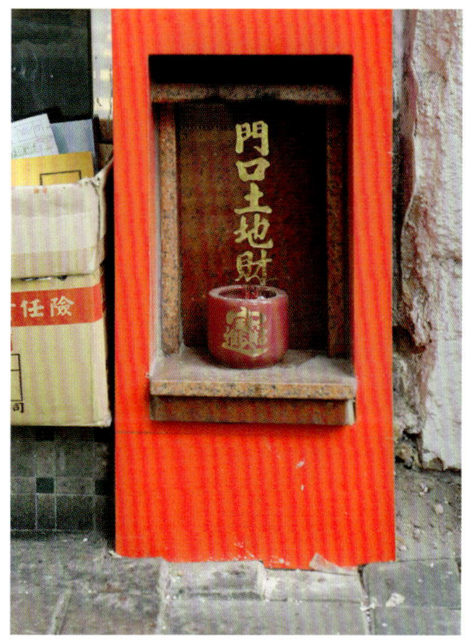

328 Shanghai Street
Yau Ma Tei, Kowloon
九龍油麻地上海街328號

Ricky Lau is a rare young face among the Earth God worshippers.

Despite being merely in his 20s, Lau talked like an expert when asked about the worshipping routines.

"We offer the Earth God three incense two times a day—in the morning and in the evening," Lau said, motioning towards the shrine sitting comfortably facing a less-than-busy street.

Bonham Strand West, perhaps better known to locals as Nam Pak Hong (North South Trade) Street, is dotted with shops selling expensive Chinese delicacies, such as ginseng, bird's nests and dried abalone. In the bygone era, it was a centre of Hong Kong's thriving entrepôt trade, hence its nickname of linking the north and the south.

"There are many things one should observe when worshipping the Earth God," Lau continued. "On the first and the 15th day of the lunar month, we present the Earth God with fruits and other offerings. Also, the shrine can get dirty over time as it's placed outdoors, so we try to clean it every few months."

Judging from the familiarity Lau displayed and the fondness he showed the shrine, it would be easy to jump to the erroneous conclusion that he is a veteran worshipper.

In fact, he only started worshipping the Earth God shrine when hired by the dried seafood shop a few months ago.

"I am a Catholic," he said. "Never have I ever worshipped a traditional Chinese deity before."

But Lau said he found no contradiction to his faith.

"It is merely a custom to respect," he said. "It's just like we have to put on a tie when we go to work, and clock out when we leave."

The young employee said his bosses are second-generation worshippers of the Earth God.

"The shrine is like a security guard of their hearts," he said. "Worshipping him makes them feel protected against evil. In the Earth God's presence, the bosses feel that no bad luck can enter the shop."

The dried seafood shop is Lau's first employer to list worshipping deities among his job duties, but Lau said it is not exactly unusual.

"I have worked in international companies before and they celebrate Christmas every year," he said. "I see Christmas dinners as the same as worshipping the Earth God—it shows respect for culture and tradition."

Lau said he was happy to honour the Earth God.

"Selling dried seafood is a traditional business, and worshipping the Earth God is an important element of it," he said.

在眾多參拜土地公公的善信之中，
劉先生該算是較年輕的一位。

還未至而立之年，劉先生已如數家珍地
把祭祀過程娓娓道來。

「我們早晚各上香一次，每次三炷香。」

樂陶陶位處的文咸西街，又名南北
行街。顧名思義，這裡曾經是香港轉口
貿易的中心，匯通南北。時至今日，
文咸西街的繁盛雖然大不如前，但仍
是不少參茸海味鋪的集中地，人參、
燕窩、鮑魚等貴價補品應有盡有。

劉先生看了看守在門口的土地公公，
繼續解釋拜祭時要注意的事項。

「除了每日上香外，每逢初一、十五
我們都會供奉水果及其他祭品。
另一方面，由於神位在路邊容易積
塵，我們至少幾個月會抹一次。」

劉先生對祭祀的熟悉，很容易令人
誤以為他是個虔誠善信。其實，他只是
幾個月前才受聘於樂陶陶，並剛開始
拜祭土地公公。

「我本身是天主教徒，以前從沒有
拜神經驗。」

但他不認為拜神和他的宗教有任何
衝突。

「我尊重傳統儀式，這是祖先定下
的規矩，就像上班要結領帶、下班要
『打卡』一樣。」

劉先生說老闆的上一代已開始拜
土地，對他們來說，土地公公是
「心靈上的保安」。「他們希望土地
會看門口，保祐大家出入平安。」

劉先生以往在外資公司工作，從來
沒有需要拜神，但他卻認為中外傳統
其實有相似之處。

「這裡會拜神、會吃開年飯，而外國
公司每年則有聖誕大餐，其實都是一樣
——尊重傳統文化。」

能夠守護中國傳統，劉先生覺得很
榮幸。

「海味店是傳統行業，祭祀尤其重要。」

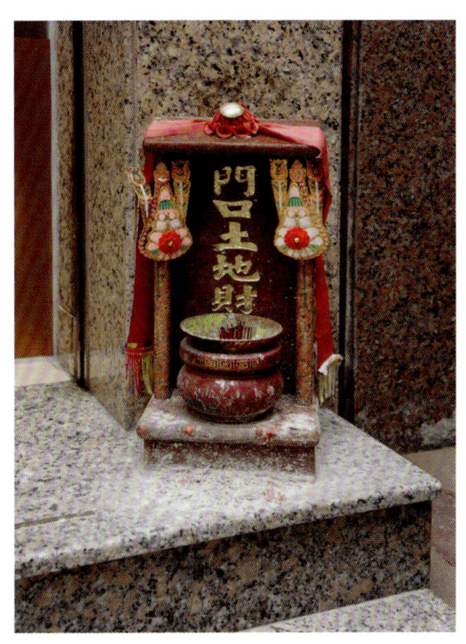

6 Bonham Strand West
Sheung Wan, Hong Kong Island
香港島上環文咸西街6號

Tin Bo is an incense shop on busy Queen's Road West. The faint smell of incense immediately soothes the mind the moment one steps into the outlet.

The Earth God, standing inside a deep pink grotto, overlooks the hustle and bustle on the major thoroughfare amid the melting summer heat.

"He's been here since the days of my father," said 59-year-old R. Tai, the second-generation owner of the shop.

For more than three decades, the Tais have been offering incense to the Earth God two times a day—in the morning and in the evening. On traditional festivals such as Mid-Autumn and Tuen Ng (Dragon Boat Festival), they also offer paper gold and silver.

"I am just following the footsteps of my father," said Tai. "It doesn't really matter whether the Earth God is indeed protecting us from evil or not."

As the protector of a traditional incense shop, the Tin Bo Earth God is luckier than most of his peers—the shrine is cleaned every day, with ashes carefully swept away and surfaces meticulously wiped.

"While most people clean the shrines every two weeks or so, we want our shrine to appear brand new every single day. There's no excuse for an incense shop to keep a dirty shrine," Tai said.

Tai said the Earth God is ranked "second class" among deities—he is considered less powerful than Guan Di and Guan Yin, but more prestigious than ancestors.

"Guan Di gets fruit offerings every day, whereas the Earth God only gets fruit during festivals," he said.

The Earth God may have protected the shop over the years, but he has not always managed to save himself from peril. Tai said the censer had been stolen twice in the past three years.

"The censer is made of metal, perhaps that's why the thieves thought it's worth some money," he said. "We now screw it firmly to the ground."

Having manned the incense shop for over three decades, Tai has witnessed many changes.

"Customers are getting older. Most of them are now over 50. Young people rarely come by, unless they are shopping for their parents," he said.

He said most customers buy incense for three deities: Guan Di, Guan Yin and the Earth God. Some customers keep more than six shrines and have to burn 30 incense every day.

In recent years, the shop welcomes one new source of customers—tourists.

"With more hotels opening in the area, more tourists are dropping by," he said. "I have Italians, Germans, etc. They like the smell of incense and love buying a small packet as a souvenir."

Tai said while he duly observes the traditions, he does not expect his sons and daughters to do the same. "Worshipping is for the sake of personal comfort. Since I've been doing this for all my life, I will continue to do so."

天寶香莊在皇后大道西開業至今，
已經三十多年了。甫踏進店內，一縷輕
輕的香燭氣就撲鼻而來。

香莊的土地公公安坐於一個深紅的
神位內，在炎炎夏日，見盡大道上的
熙來攘往。

戴先生是香莊的第二代傳人，他說
土地公公在父親掌鋪時已屹立於此。

三十多年來，香莊的老少上下都風雨
不改，為土地公公早晚各上一炷香。
每逢初一、十五，又或是中秋、端午，
他們更會奉上金銀元寶。

「我只是跟傳統，一向這樣做，也無
所謂『靈不靈』。」

天寶的土地公公比同儕幸運，每天都有
專人打掃抹淨、清理香灰。

「我們是香燭店，當然要保持門面
亮麗。有人初一、十五才打掃，我們就
堅持每天打理。」

香莊內有不同大小的香燭，戴先生說
最好的香通常奉予大神，而奉予
祖先的通常比較次一等。「土地不及
關帝和觀音，但又比祖先高一等。
關公每天都有人奉上水果祭品，但土地
過節時才會有。」

縱然土地公公為香莊擋去不少邪靈
霉氣，但有時卻自身難保。戴先生
說大約兩至三年前，香爐曾兩次被盜。

「香爐用金屬打造，可能賊人見變賣
有價，便乘機偷去。所以我們現在已用
螺絲上緊，不能隨便拾起。」

戴先生自小就在香莊幫忙，覺得多年來
有不少變化。

「現在的客人通常是老一輩，年輕人
較少，除非是幫父母買東西。」

他說顧客通常供奉關帝、觀音及土地。
有些善信家中有六七個神位，每天
要上超過三十支香。

近年，香莊開拓了新的客源——遊客。

「他們多住在附近新落成的酒店，
經過便順道買一兩包作手信。我見過
意大利人、德國人等，他們說喜歡
香燭的氣味。」

戴先生雖然自己堅守傳統，但他不
期望子女會跟隨。

「拜神只為求心安，我已拜了這麼
多年，一定會繼續拜下去。」

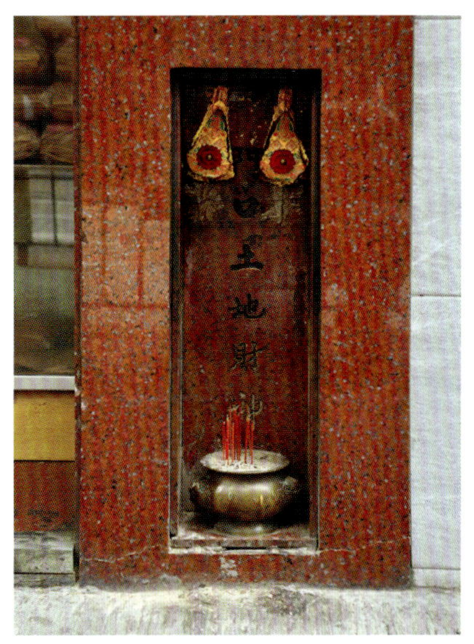

273 Queen's Road West
Sheung Wan, Hong Kong Island
香港島上環皇后大道西街273號

Surrounded by the many eateries and restaurants on Ivy Street, the Hong Mei Hair Salon has at least one thing in common with them—it has an Earth God guarding the shopfront with solemnity and vigour.

The salon is a small business in the neighbourhood of Tai Kok Tsui, developed decades ago as a residential haven for the booming population of Hong Kong.

Ivy Street, one of the 20 streets in the area that are named after plants, has recently become a food street lined with local specialties.

Besides the shrine, the salon is adorned by many Fai Chun and posters of the Wealth God. But Sito Kin-lung, who owns the little salon near Cosmopolitan Estate, said he actually did not know why one should worship the Earth God.

"I am just following the advice of my family elders," he said. "They told me to install an Earth God altar when I opened the shop. I did it because everyone else was doing it."

Like other worshippers, Sito tries to worship the Earth God every morning and every evening with incense. However, it is not his habit to offer anything special during festivities.

"Sometimes I forget to offer him incense," he said. "But I think it is fine. The Earth God will not get angry—he must be more open-minded than we mortals are!"

As the shrine stands right beside a busy street with plenty of traffic, the hairdresser said he cleans it every two weeks with a wet cloth. When he is not around, his two staff members help.

Although there are posters of other gods on the walls, the salon only worships the Earth God. Sito said it was again on the advice of his elders.

"They said the mere presence of the Earth God was enough. As long as he stands at the entrance to block away all evil spirits and bad luck, there is no need for other gods to be here," he said.

Sito said he believed that the Earth God was indeed powerful, even if his power was only limited to the local neighbourhood. "If he was not doing a good job to shut out evil spirits, there would not be so many people who continue to worship him."

The owner did not find worshipping the Earth God anything special, as almost every single shop on the street was doing the same.

"The Earth God protects all businesses, not just hair salons," he said. "As long as a shop opens itself to the public, it falls under the Earth God's jurisdiction."

He said while he is not a religious or superstitious person, he enjoys making the worship of the Earth God a daily habit.

"I guess it brings a certain degree of comfort to me," he said. "The Earth God is said to shield us from bad luck. That way, I can carry on with my work at ease."

埃華街是大角咀區內新興的食街。
在芸芸食肆中，康美髮型屋至少
有一樣東西和其他商鋪相同，就是
它們都供奉土地財神。

髮型屋位於舊區大角咀。上世紀
五六十年代，大角咀逐漸發展成新興
的住宅區，吸引不少新移民遷入。

埃華街是區內二十條以植物命名的
街道之一，音譯自長春藤 (Ivy)。

除了門口土地財神外，髮型屋裡面
掛滿揮春紅紙，寓意大吉大利。老闆
司徒先生卻老實地承認，其實他
不太明白為何要拜神。

「老人家說要拜，我也是聽從他們。
我開業時，他們著我別忘記預留
位置供奉土地，我看見其他人都拜，
便跟著做。」

像其他善信一般，司徒先生盡量每天
早晚各上一炷香。但初一、十五
的時候，他卻不會特別準備其他祭品。

「記得的時候我便上香，不記得也
沒所謂。土地公公很大方，不會像
凡人般隨便動怒的。」

神位面對著馬路，容易積塵，司徒先生
會每兩週用濕布抹一次。有時他有
其他事要辦，他的兩名員工也會幫忙。

雖然店內有不少財神海報，髮型屋就
只供奉土地公公一個。

「老人家說有土地守門口已經足夠。只
要沒有霉運走進來，便不需要其他
神祇。」

司徒先生相信土地公公「應該很靈」，
若非如此，「應該吸引不了這麼多人
繼續拜祭」。

他說整條街的商鋪都拜土地，絕不是
甚麼特別習俗。

「打開門做生意便需要土地保祐，
又豈止我們髮型屋。」

雖然司徒先生不認為自己迷信，但他
卻樂於每天拜土地。

「這是心靈安慰，霉運遠去了，做事
也安心點。」

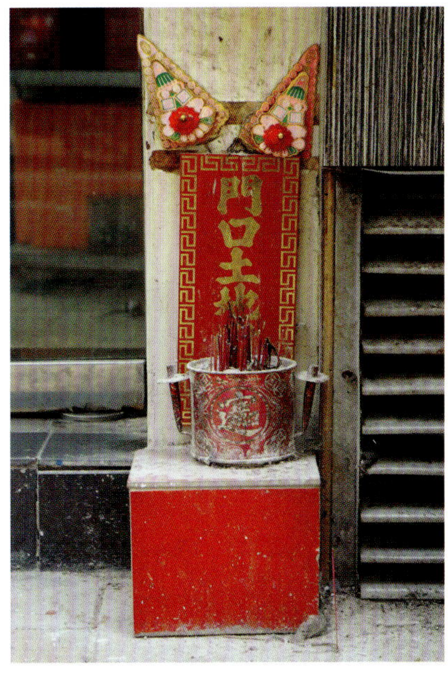

Shop A2, 101 Ivy Street
Tai Kok Tsui, Kowloon
九龍大角咀埃華街101號地下A2鋪位

Custodian: **Ms. Lee Yung**, custodian of the Shum family's Earth God worship customs and tradition. Lee's late husband ran a family manufacturing and wholesale business in curry and pepper powder condiments. Below are some of the main Earth God practices described by her:

(A) Installing an Earth God shrine

1. Find a suitable place outside the residence by the side of the doorway.
2. Get an Earth God tablet (of wood or fibreboard).
3. Boil several pomelo leaves in clean water (tap water will do), and cleanse the tablet with a clean towel wet with the pomelo water, then dry the tablet with another clean towel.
4. Get a red sash (this is a piece of red cloth of about two inches wide, with the centre knotted into a ball) and drape it around the top and sides of the tablet.
5. Get an incense urn and fill it with white bone ash, and place it in front of the tablet.
6. Prepare offerings: three cups of wine; three cups of tea; three bowls of cooked rice; a cooked chicken; a large piece of roasted pork; four oranges or tangerines.
7. Other offerings: a pair of candles; three joss-sticks; two portions of paper sycees (a portion is two pieces); joss-papers; burn all of them and the process is completed.

(B) Relocating an Earth God shrine

If a shrine is to be moved to a new home, one only needs to verbally invite the Earth God to follow along. If a shrine is no longer needed because of emigration or other reasons, then the Earth God shrine has to be relocated to a temple or under an old banyan tree.

(C) Sealing an Earth God shrine

If the ash of a deceased family member is to be brought home, the shrine must first be temporarily sealed with red paper. Otherwise the spirit of the deceased will be blocked outside the doorway and become a wandering ghost. The shrine can only be unsealed after the ash of the deceased has been properly placed in its own shrine.

(D) Paying respect to the Earth God on special occasions

Respect must be paid to the Earth God (with the same offerings used in the shrine installation) on major festivals, in particular the god's birthday on the second day of the second Chinese lunar month, in order to keep the home spiritually safe. This is because the Earth God is the first line of defence at the doorway against the intrusion of ghosts and evil spirits.

李蓉女士，岑家拜土地傳統習俗的承傳人。李女士的亡夫生前經營家族生意，專門製造和批發咖哩粉及胡椒粉等調味品。以下根據李女士描述的拜土地規矩：

（甲）土地神位的安置

1. 先在住宅門外旁邊找個合適的位置。
2. 買神位牌（可選用木或纖維板製造的）。
3. 把幾片柚子葉放在清水中煲滾（自來水便可），然後用乾淨毛巾沾濕柚子水為神位牌潔身，再用乾毛巾抹乾。
4. 買神紅（這是一條約兩英吋寬的紅色布帶，中間用原布條捲造成花球形狀），圍在神位的上方及左右方。
5. 買香爐及白牙灰，放在神位前。
6. 準備祭品：燒酒三杯、茶三杯、飯三碗、一隻熟雞、一大塊燒肉、四個橙或桔。
7. 其他祭品：香燭一對、三支香、元寶（兩塊為一份，最少兩份）、金銀衣紙，全部燒給土地神便完成。

（乙）土地神位的搬移

如因搬家而搬移神位，只需品神土地，邀請他跟隨到新居處。如因移民或其他原因而不需要土地神，就請土地神移位到廟堂或老榕樹腳下。

（丙）土地神位的封存

如有家人過身，骨灰需要暫時帶回家，首先用紅紙暫封神位，才可把骨灰帶入屋，否則亡靈會被阻擋門外不能歸家，成為孤魂野鬼。骨灰安置於龕位後才可以解封。

（丁）特別節日時土地神的拜祭

所有大時大節，尤其是農曆二月初二的土地誕，都不可不拜土地，因為所有妖魔鬼怪都要先經過門口才可進入屋中，土地是第一防綫，所以要拜土地以保祐家宅平安。

Biography

Michael Wolf was born in 1954 in Munich, Germany. He grew up in the United States, Europe and Canada, and studied at UC Berkeley and the Folkwang School in Essen, Germany. In 1995 Michael Wolf moved to Hong Kong, where he studied intensively Chinese cultural identity and the complex urban architectural structure. He has published seven photobooks to this date on Asia: *China im Wandel* (Frederking und Thaler, 2001), *Sitting in China* (Steidl, 2002), *Chinese Propaganda Posters* (Taschen, 2003), *Hong Kong Front Door Back Door* (Thames & Hudson, 2005), *Hong Kong Inside Outside* (Asia One/Peperoni Books, 2009), *Tokyo Compression* (Asia One/Peperoni Books, 2010) and *Hong Kong Corner Houses* (Hong Kong University Press, 2011).

Dr. Lee Ho Yin is the Director of the Architectural Conservation Programmes (ACP) at The University of Hong Kong (HKU); he is a well-known academic and practitioner in the field of heritage conservation in Hong Kong.

Prof. Lynne D. DiStefano is a Past Director and current Adjunct Professor of ACP; on behalf of the International Council on Monuments and Sites (ICOMOS), she carries out missions related to proposed or inscribed World Heritage Sites.

Katie Cummer is an Academic Tutor for ACP and the Coordinator of Teaching and Research; she is currently studying for her PhD at HKU.

Sandy Shum Wai Yee is at present studying for a BA (Hons) in Business Enterprise at University College Birmingham, University of Birmingham.

作者簡介　**吳爾夫**於1954年出生在德國慕尼黑，在美國、歐洲與加拿大長大，求學於著名的美國 UC Berkeley 大學與德國 Folkwang 學院 (現今改稱為 Folkwang University of the Arts)。他在1995年移居到香港，從而熟悉了中國的文化認同與大都市中錯綜複雜的建築。他至今共出版了七本以亞洲為題材的攝影集：*China im Wandel* (Frederking und Thaler, 2001)，*Sitting in China* (Steidl, 2002)，*Chinese Propaganda Posters* (Taschen, 2003)，*Hong Kong Front Door Back Door* (Thames & Hudson, 2005)，《香港裡外》(Asia One/Peperoni Books, 2009)，*Tokyo Compression* (Asia One/Peperoni Books, 2010) 和《街頭街尾》(Hong Kong University Press, 2011)。

李浩然博士，現任香港大學建築文物保護課程主任，是香港著名的文物保育學者與專家。

狄麗玲教授，香港大學建築文物保護課程前主任，現任該課程的客席教授，她被「國際古蹟遺址理事會」委任為聯合國教科文組織世界文化遺產技術評審員。

康嘉玲，現任香港大學建築文物保護課程的學術導師與課程兼研究統籌，她亦是香港大學的博士研究生。

岑慧儀，現正在英國伯明翰大學學院攻讀工商企業管理（榮譽）文學士學位。